# Does the Bible Tell Me So?

# Does the Bible Tell Me So?

Margaret Nutting Ralph

WITHDRAWN

ROWMAN & LITTLEFIELD
Lanham • Boulder • New York • London

Published by Rowman & Littlefield
An imprint of The Rowman & Littlefield Publishing Group, Inc.
4501 Forbes Boulevard, Suite 200, Lanham, Maryland 20706
https://rowman.com

6 Tinworth Street, London SE11 5AL, United Kingdom

British Library Cataloguing in Publication Information Available

**Library of Congress Cataloging-in-Publication Data**

Names: Ralph, Margaret Nutting, author.
Title: Does the Bible tell me so? / Margaret Nutting Ralph.
Description: Lanham : Rowman & Littlefield Publishing Group, Inc., 2019. |
    Includes bibliographical references and index.
Identifiers: LCCN 2019011549 | ISBN 9781538129609 (cloth : alk. paper)
Subjects: LCSH: Bible--Criticism, interpretation, etc.
Classification: LCC BS511.3 .R35 2019 | DDC 220.6--dc23 LC record available at https://
    lccn.loc.gov/2019011549

This book is dedicated to two gifted scholars, teachers, and authors:

Raymond Brown, who taught us to understand the meaning, the wisdom, the revelation in Scripture.

Teilhard de Chardin, who taught us to see the innate unity and holiness in all of creation, especially in all human beings.

Each helped us better understand how we are to live and who we are called to become, thus making us more attentive to Jesus's words: "By this everyone will know that you are my disciples, if you have love for one another." (John 13:35)

# Contents

# Acknowledgments

In my previous books, my acknowledgments have thanked fellow professionals in religious education, publishers who helped me along the way, and family and friends who supported me. These acknowledgments are different. I wrote three-fourths of this book four years ago. Three years ago my husband, Don, whom in previous books I have always thanked for his love and unfailing support, suffered a traumatic brain injury. Wonderful health-care workers at Baptist Health and at Cardinal Hill Rehabilitation Hospital in Lexington, Kentucky, nursed him back to health over two years of patient and loving care. My deepest gratitude goes to each and every one of them. In addition, I would like to thank Sarah Stanton, my first editor at Rowman & Littlefield, and Rolf Janke, my present editor at Rowman & Littlefield, for their continued interest in this project despite my long delay in completing it. Thank you, one and all, for helping to make *Does the Bible Tell Me So?* become a reality.

# Introduction

First Verse:

> Jesus loves me. This I know,
> For the Bible tells me so;
> Little ones to him belong,
> They are weak, but he is strong.

Refrain:

> Yes, Jesus loves me.
> Yes, Jesus loves me.
> Yes, Jesus loves me.
> The Bible tells me so.

This first verse of the poem *Jesus Loves Me*, by Anna Bartlett Warner (1860), and the refrain, written by William Batchelder Bradbury when he turned the poem into a hymn (1862), make up one of the most beloved and well-known children's songs throughout the English-speaking, Christian world.

"The Bible tells me so." One might think that this statement would settle many an argument for Christians who accept the authority of the Bible. However, it doesn't. Why not? Because Christians do not all agree on how to interpret the Bible. Some totally committed Christians are fundamentalists: they do not always consider context when determining meaning. Other totally committed Christians are contextualists: they do consider context before determining meaning. This difference in method of interpretation leads to a difference in conclusions, a difference in beliefs about what the Bible actually teaches.

The division between fundamentalists and contextualists is not a disagreement about whether Scripture is revelation, biblical authors are inspired, or Scripture is a living word that can cut to the marrow of the bone. The disagreement is simply about how to interpret Scripture so as to correctly understand the revelation that both fundamentalists and contextualists claim is there.

The fundamentalist/contextualist controversy is not a disagreement between denominations, but within each denomination. Even if a church officially teaches the contextualist method of interpretation, as does the Catholic Church (see the Second Vatican Council document *Dei Verbum*), that does not mean that all members of that church know and follow this teaching.

The topic of how to interpret Scripture so as to correctly understand what it teaches is extremely important, not only for denominational unity and unity among Christian denominations, but for civil dialogue and peaceful decision making in our local communities, our states, and our countries. This issue has been of great importance in the past, is now, and will continue to be important in the future. It is an undeniable fact of history that the Bible has been used to support practices that very few of us would support today, such as validating slavery or denying women the right to vote. Surely, we do not want to make that same mistake today when discussing contemporary civil rights issues.

It is my own belief that we could have avoided abusing Scripture in the past, and we could avoid abusing Scripture in the present and in the future, simply by asking ourselves a simple question: Is the inspired author I am quoting when I use Scripture to make a point addressing the same topic that I am using the passage to address? If the answer is no, then we should not use that passage to add authority to our own conclusions.

How are we to determine the intent of the original inspired author? In order to correctly discern what the author is teaching, we must consider his words within several contexts: the literary form or kind of writing that the author has chosen to use, the beliefs at the time of the original author and audience, and the two thousand-year process of ongoing revelation that is modeled for us in Scripture.

In this book, I will first briefly explain each of the three contexts that we must consider in order to understand a biblical author's intent. I will then apply this method of interpretation to some historical issues, demonstrating just how the Bible was abused to support the deep-seated prejudices of well-meaning people. Since most readers will agree on these issues, they will more readily understand that the biblical texts were misused. With this knowledge firmly in hand, I will then turn to some contemporary issues, applying the same method of interpretation, in order to examine if Scripture is being used or abused in these contexts.

In addition to addressing topics where the answer to the question "Does the Bible tell me so?" will be no, I will examine some topics where the answer will be yes. Obviously, it is at least as important to know what the Bible does teach as it is to know what the Bible does not teach.

After all, none of us who treasure the Bible and accept its authority want to abuse it. We treasure the Bible because we believe it is revelatory of God's truth and God's will. When we correctly interpret a biblical text, we use it to correctly discern how God would have us live our lives so as to cooperate with the coming of God's kingdom. When we incorrectly interpret a biblical text, using it to proof text our own prejudices, we disobey the second commandment, which says: "You shall not make wrongful use of the name of the Lord your God . . . " (Ex 20:7).

Many people think this commandment is simply forbidding swearing. I agree with those who think its meaning is much broader than that. In this commandment, God is also instructing God's people not to misuse God's name by claiming that God has revealed, or that God's authority is behind, a policy or practice that discriminates against any of God's beloved people. When we do that, when we use God's name to justify any kind of prejudice or discrimination, we are truly using God's name in vain.

After all, the words *Jesus loves me* are true no matter who is saying them. Therefore, the way we treat any other person is the way we are treating a beloved child of God. I will demonstrate the truth of these statements in a future chapter. Why am I confident that these spiritual insights are true? The Bible, when read in context, does tell me so.

*Chapter One*

# Considering Context

Why is it that two people who have both turned to the Bible as a source of revelation and claim, "The Bible tells me so," can, at the same time, totally disagree on an issue? Does the Bible contradict itself, or are people abusing biblical texts, claiming that the Bible teaches something that it does not teach?

Very often, the reason is the latter. Instead of allowing the Bible to form their thinking, people often approach the Bible with their minds already made up. Instead of reading a whole book of the Bible, so that they understand what the inspired author is speaking about, they take individual sentences out of context and use them to add support to their previously formed opinions. Such an approach is called "proof texting." The goal of proof texting is to add authority to one's own opinions, not to seek to know what God has revealed to God's people.

In order to understand what biblical authors are teaching, one must put individual sentences in the context in which they appear in the Bible. The three contexts that we must consider are the literary form of the book in which the passage appears, the beliefs and presumptions shared by the author and his audience, and where in the process of revelation the author's insights belong. In other words, we must ask ourselves: Is this insight one step on the road to truth, or does this insight represent the fullness of truth?

## LITERARY FORM

We are all familiar with the concept of *literary form*, even though we may not consciously think about it or be able to name various kinds of writing. For instance, when we read a story in which a turtle and a rabbit have a conversation, we may not know that the name of this literary form is *fable* or

1

that the literary device being used when animals talk just like human beings is *personification*, but we do know that we are not reading history or a scientific text. When we read an editorial, we know that we are not reading objective, well-balanced reporting, and we give the author permission to try to persuade us to his or her point of view. We do this because we know that to persuade, not simply to inform, is the function of an editorial.

This same concept holds true for the Bible. The books in the library that we call the *Bible* are written in a variety of literary forms. If we fail to consider form, simply presuming that every author's intent is to describe events as we would have witnessed them had we been present, we will nearly always misunderstand what the inspired authors intended to teach.

People who neglect to consider literary form when trying to determine meaning in biblical passages are prone to make one of two mistakes. The first mistake is that they misunderstand what an inspired author is saying on the topic under discussion. The second is that they misunderstand the topic, change the subject, and act as though Scripture speaks definitively on subjects that no inspired biblical author addressed in the first place. Examples of each of these mistakes will make the essential importance of considering literary form clear.

## AN EXAMPLE OF BEING ON
## THE WRONG SIDE OF THE TOPIC

Say two people are arguing over why people suffer. One firmly believes that all suffering is punishment for sin. He thinks that if a person is suffering, he or she must deserve it. To prove his point, he looks for a passage of Scripture that appears to agree with him. He finds the passage he is looking for in the book of Job. Since the words he is quoting are in the Bible, and since he believes that God is ultimately the author of the Bible, he attributes the following words to God:

> Think now, who that was innocent ever perished?
> Or where were the upright cut off?
> As I have seen, those who plow iniquity
> and sow trouble reap the same. (Job 3:7–8)

Being firm in his conviction, and now having proven that God agrees with him, this person's way of "comforting" a suffering person is judgmental and threatening: repent before something even worse happens to you.

Now, if this person considered the context of literary form, he would come to a very different conclusion. Instead of using Scripture to support what he already thinks, he would read the whole book of Job to determine what the author intended to teach.

Most of the book of Job, the parts written in poetry (Chapters 3–41), is a debate about whether all suffering is punishment for sin. When one reads the book, one understands that various points of view are being presented, as is always true in a debate. The passage quoted above is not said by God, but by a participant in the debate named Eliphaz. As the debate concludes, God enters the debate and says that Eliphaz is wrong: ". . . the Lord said to Eliphaz the Temanite: 'My wrath is kindled against you and against your two friends; for you have not spoken of me what is right . . .'" (Job 42:7b). Eliphaz has taken God's name in vain.

Had the person presenting his views read the book of Job to form his opinions rather than looking for a single sentence that, taken out of context, seemed to support his views, he would not have misquoted Scripture. He would not have taken God's name in vain. Instead, he would have understood that the author is teaching that suffering *is not* always punishment for sin, the very opposite of what the person used the out-of-context passage to teach.

## AN EXAMPLE OF CHANGING
## THE TOPIC ALTOGETHER

Many people who fail to consider literary form use the Bible to address topics that biblical authors aren't addressing. This is the mistake that people are making when they try to use biblical texts to give authoritative answers to scientific questions. All biblical authors lived in a pre-scientific age. No biblical author is trying to answer a scientific question. Instead, biblical authors are addressing questions that are crucial to our spiritual lives, questions such as: Who is God? Who are we, communally and individually? Why do we suffer? How should we live so as to be in right relationship with God and with each other? What is our destiny?

Again, an example will make this point clear. Some biblical fundamentalists claim that the earth is about six thousand years old. To support this view, they count six days from creation to Adam, based on the first chapters of Genesis. They then calculate the years between Adam and Abraham, based on genealogies, and the years from Abraham to the present age. The problem with this argument is that it ignores the context of literary form.

The first stories in Genesis are not addressing the question: How much time elapsed between the creation of the earth and the appearance of the first human beings? How do we know? —Because the literary form of the creation in six days and the story of Adam and Eve is obviously not historical or scientific writing. History is about events that have been witnessed and about which we have oral or written accounts. No human being witnessed creation. Human beings do not even appear in the story until the sixth day. Nor are the stories examples of scientific writing. We can tell this because the inspired author has used personification: he makes a snake talk. Obviously, these stories are imaginative and symbolic stories teaching truths about our spiritual lives, not about scientific facts.

We will discuss what truths the inspired authors are teaching in a later chapter. For now it suffices to say that to treat the stories as scientific or historical accounts and to seek scientific or historical answers in them is to change the subject entirely. We are no longer talking about our spiritual lives. We are no longer benefiting from what the inspired authors intended to teach us.

## THE BELIEFS OF THE TIME OF THE AUTHOR
## AND THE ORIGINAL AUDIENCE

The second context we must consider in order to correctly understand the revelation that inspired biblical authors are teaching is the context of the author's and the original audience's beliefs. We put the authority of Scripture behind what the authors are teaching on the topics they are addressing, not behind their presumptions on other, unrelated topics or behind their applications of core truths to their particular social settings.

## PRESUMPTIONS ON UNRELATED TOPICS

No biblical author teaches us about the shape of the earth. That is a scientific, not spiritual, topic. However, in the course of teaching spiritual topics, such as the relationship between God and the created order, authors picture God making the earth in the shape that they presumed the earth to be. Biblical authors, who lived in a pre-scientific age, presumed that the earth was flat, had a dome over it, and rested on posts.

That is why the author of the creation story says, "And God said, 'Let there be a dome in the midst of the waters, and let it separate the waters from the waters.' So God made the dome and separated the waters that were under the dome from the waters that were above the dome. And it was so. God called the dome Sky" (Gen 1:6–8).

That is why the author of Job pictures God asking Job: "Where were you when I laid the foundations of the earth? / Tell me, if you have understanding. / Who determined its measurements—surely you know! / Or who stretched the line upon it? / On what were its bases sunk, / or who laid its cornerstone . . . " (Job 38:4–6)?

The fact that the inspired authors did not know anything more about the shape of the earth than did their generation does not in any way challenge the belief that they were inspired and that their stories are teaching eternal truths that every generation needs to hear. Presuming that the earth is flat does not affect one's relationship with God in one way or another. Believing that God is the source of one's being and that God is loving has a profound effect on one's self-concept and on one's ways of acting. The authors were inspired on the topics they were addressing, and those topics were spiritual topics, not scientific topics.

Along with not putting the authority of Scripture behind presumptions of the time, we do not put the authority of Scripture behind applications of core truths to particular social settings. This is the mistake that many people made when they used Scripture to justify slavery, a topic we will discuss in more detail in Chapter 2.

For example, the letter to the Ephesians says: "Slaves, obey your earthly masters with fear and trembling, in singleness of heart, as you obey Christ . . . " (Eph 6:5). This passage was used to support slavery. However, the passage is not teaching the core truth that the author is teaching. Rather, it is an application of that core truth to a particular social setting. The core truth precedes this statement: "Therefore be imitators of God, as beloved children, and live in love, as Christ loved us and gave himself up for us, a fragrant offering and sacrifice to God" (Eph 5:1–2).

The author of Ephesians is writing a letter (a specific literary form) to a particular audience (the Ephesians). The social setting of the audience is a given: slaves are the property of their masters. The eternal spiritual truth that is being taught is that we must love every other person as a beloved child of God. The application of that truth to this particular social setting does not question the social order but applies the truth to that social order. It tells masters how to treat their slaves lovingly, and it tells slaves how to treat their masters lovingly. The author does not question, nor condone, the social order. Therefore, to use this passage to answer the question, "Is slavery as it was practiced in the United States moral or immoral?" is an abuse of Scripture. It is using a passage of Scripture to address a question that the inspired author was not addressing. If used in support of slavery, it is taking God's name in vain.

## A TWO THOUSAND YEAR PROCESS OF REVELATION

The third context that we must consider is the fact that the Bible models a two thousand year process of coming to knowledge, not a collection of bottom-line answers that we can quote to prove we are right. This process began around the time of Abraham (1850 BC) and ended in the early second century AD. Over those two thousand years, people grew in their understanding. So, an early inspired author might say something that is true, something that is a growth in understanding for his generation, but something that is a partial truth, not a whole truth. Later generations, standing on the shoulders of their ancestors, build on that truth and reach an even fuller truth.

People who do not understand this often think that the Bible contradicts itself. They compare an early insight to a later insight and think of them as contradictory rather than as steps in a process of coming to a fuller knowledge. I once had a conversation with such a person. After first meeting, she asked me, "What do you do?" I said, "I teach Scripture." She laughed boisterously and said, "Well, good luck! First it says, 'An eye for an eye and a tooth for a tooth.' Then it says, 'Love, your enemy.' I say, take your pick."

This woman was correct in saying that first the Bible says "an eye for an eye." In Exodus we read: "If any harm follows, then you shall give life for life, eye for eye, tooth for tooth, hand for hand, foot for foot, burn for burn, wound for wound, stripe for stripe" (Ex 21:23–25). This law dates to the time of Moses, about 1250 BC, and is a step forward in teaching the ramifications of the fact that God is love. The teaching is against blind revenge; it is demanding a measured response to injury. The Israelites must not do worse to a person who has injured them than that person did to them.

The woman was also correct in saying, "Then it says, 'Love your enemy.'" This is a quotation from Jesus's Sermon on the Mount in Matthew's Gospel. Jesus begins by quoting Exodus: "You have heard that it was said, 'An eye for an eye and a tooth for a tooth.'" Jesus then goes on, not to deny that truth, but to build on it. Jesus says, "But I say to you, do not resist an evildoer. But if anyone strikes you on the right cheek, turn the other also. . . . Love your enemies and pray for those who persecute you" (Matt 5:38–39, 44). Jesus did not come to abolish the law and the prophets, but to fulfill them (see Matt 5:17).

In teaching his disciples to love their enemies, Jesus is not saying that his ancestors in faith were wrong. It is true that one should not act in anger, seeking revenge and hoping to abolish an enemy. However, this insight was a step on the way to truth, a partial truth, not the whole truth. The whole truth is that God loves everyone, and Jesus's disciples are to reflect God's love to everyone, even to their enemies.

The Bible reflects a gradual coming to knowledge over the centuries in regard to many questions relevant to our spiritual lives, relevant to our relationship with God and with each other. So the woman was not correct when she concluded, "Take your pick," between early and later insights. To take a partial truth and present it as the whole truth, as the fullness of revelation, is one more way to misrepresent what the Bible teaches. It is one more way to take God's name in vain.

In future chapters we will apply this contextualist approach to many passages of Scripture. To answer the question, "Does the Bible tell me so?" in regard to a variety of claims, we will put the passages in question in the context in which they appear in the Bible. Only when we consider the literary form in which each passage appears, when we ask ourselves if this is a core truth or something the author has said by way of example or application, and when we ask ourselves where this insight comes in the two thousand-year process of revelation will we be able to answer the question accurately. Only then can we claim, "The Bible tells me so."

## Chapter Two

# Slavery Is Moral

## *Does the Bible Tell Me So?*
## *No*

We will now apply our contextualist method of interpreting the Bible to a topic on which I think we have reached agreement. People in the twenty-first century no longer defend slavery. Christians no longer use the Bible to support slavery, and those who did so in the past have now apologized for that error. Since we now agree on this topic, we can look at the way the Bible was used to support slavery, in order to demonstrate the mistakes in interpretation without becoming defensive on the issue. As we will see, in every instance, an out-of-context biblical passage was used to support what advocates for slavery already believed. In doing so, no consideration was given to literary form, to the presumptions of the time, or to the process of revelation that the Bible contains. The slaveholders were not asking, "What was this inspired author teaching his audience?" They were asking, "What Scripture can I quote that will appear to support my convictions?"

### THE CLAIM: SLAVERY WAS
### ESTABLISHED BY GOD

One basic claim made by the advocates of slavery is that God established slavery as part of the social order. The foundational passage that was used to attribute the establishment of slavery directly to God was a passage from Genesis known as *Noah's curse*. Noah is pictured as saying:

> "Cursed be Canaan;
> Lowest of slaves shall he be to his brothers."

He also said,
"Blessed by the Lord my God be Shem;
And let Canaan be his slave.
May God make space for Japheth,
And let him lie in the tents of Shem;
And let Canaan be his slave." (Gen 9:25–27)

The defenders of slavery claimed that this passage, which they believed was actually spoken by Noah before slavery as an institution existed, proves that slavery was part of God's plan all along. Since slavery did come into existence after Noah's time, they claim that in hindsight we realize that Noah must have been inspired by God when he spoke these words. Therefore, God willed that some people be slaves. [1]

What mistakes lie behind this interpretation? The first mistake is a failure to consider literary form. What kind of writing are we reading? The passage in question is just one part of an extended story of Noah. So let us first put Noah's words into the context of the plot in which they appear in Genesis.

The setting is after the flood. Noah has drunk too much wine and has been seen drunk and naked in his tent by his youngest son, Ham, who told his brothers, Shem and Japheth. By doing this, Ham showed lack of proper respect for his father. Shem and Japheth did show respect. They backed into the tent and covered their father, thus not seeing his nakedness. When Noah awoke, he knew what had happened and spoke the curse quoted above (Gen 9:18–27).

Noah's son, Ham, was the father of Canaan. So, in Noah's curse, Ham's descendants, the Canaanites, were to become slaves to his brothers' descendants. Shem's descendants are the Israelites. Noah is saying that the Canaanites would become slaves of the Israelites.

Those who used Noah's curse to defend slavery as it was practiced in the United States brought several false presumptions to the story of Noah. First, they assumed that they were reading history, that the author was describing for them what they would have seen and heard had they witnessed the events described. They assumed that a historical Noah actually spoke these words, and centuries later they came true.

In addition, they assumed that the time of the author and the time of the plot were the same. So, the author knew no more about future events than did the character Noah. Both of these presumptions are in error.

The stories in the first eleven chapters of Genesis are not, by literary form, historical writing. We have already mentioned this fact in relation to the story of the man and woman in the garden in which the author of the story uses personification; he has a snake talk. Such unrealistic plot elements are evidence that the literary form being used is neither history nor science.

The plot elements in the story of Noah are also unrealistic. The author tells us that "on the very same day Noah with his sons, Shem and Ham and

Japheth, and Noah's wife and the three wives of his sons entered the ark, they and every wild animal of every kind, and all domestic animals of every kind, and every creeping thing that creeps on the earth, and every bird of every kind—every bird, every winged creature. They went into the ark with Noah, two and two of all flesh in which there was the breath of life. And those that entered, male and female of all flesh, went in as God had commanded him; and the Lord shut him in" (Gen 7:13–16).

No human being could gather two of every living creature that lives on the earth and put them on a boat. The author expects us to know that. When we read such an account, we know that we are reading a story written to teach a lesson, not an eyewitness account of events. The question we want to ask is: What about our relationship with God is the inspired author teaching us? (We will return to this question shortly.)

The presumption that the time of the author is the same as the time of Noah, before slavery was known on earth, is also a false presumption. We can tell that the time of the author is much, much later because the author includes elements in the story plot that are contemporary with his own time, not the time of the plot. For instance, Noah is told to take both clean and unclean animals. God says, "Take with you seven pairs of all clean animals, the male and its mate; and a pair of the animals that are not clean, the male and its mate. . . . " (Gen 7:2). The distinction between clean and unclean animals was first promulgated about the time of Moses (1250 BC; see Lev 11:47). Thus, this detail is contemporary with the author but not with the plot.

In fact, Scripture scholars believe that the Noah story was edited into its present version after the Babylonian exile (587–537 BC) and after the Israelites had returned to the Holy Land. At that time, because the Israelites no longer had their own king and kingdom but lived under Persian rule, the priests became their community leaders. The priests went over their inherited written and oral traditions, editing the stories into the versions that we now have, and editing the connected narrative into the order that we now have.

## WHAT IS THE AUTHOR
## TEACHING THE AUDIENCE?

The Noah story is one of the stories in the first eleven chapters of Genesis that set the stage for the call of Abraham in Chapter 12, the beginning of salvation history. The overall plot of the narrative is the creation of human beings in God's own image (Gen 1:27; 9:6) and the growth of sinfulness on the earth that made it necessary for God to step in and save God's people because they certainly could not save themselves.

Noah's story is one of four sin stories that show the constantly growing sinfulness of human beings: Adam and Eve disobey God, and Adam blames Eve for his disobedience. Cain doesn't just blame Abel; he kills him. By the time of Noah, the earth has become so sinful that God regrets having made it in the first place: "The Lord saw that the wickedness of humankind was great in the earth, and that every inclination of the thought of their hearts was only evil continually. And the Lord was sorry that he had made humankind on the earth, and it grieved him to his heart. So the Lord said, 'I will blot out from the earth the human beings I have created—people together with animals and creeping things and birds of the air, for I am sorry that I have made them'" (Gen 6:5–7).

However, because Noah has found favor with God, God changes God's mind. God decides to save Noah, his family, and the other living creatures. Notice the way God is pictured as having the traits of a human being: God gets angry but then thinks better of what God had planned to do. God won't destroy everything after all (Gen 8:21–22). Such descriptions are called *anthropomorphic* pictures of God. That the story pictures an anthropomorphic God is one more piece of evidence that we are reading a story composed to teach a lesson, not to be an eyewitness account of an event.

Although the writing in the story of Noah is neither historical nor scientific, the lesson of the story is true: Even though human beings continue to sin, God continues to save. God promises that God will not destroy what God has made in God's own image despite the fact that human beings continue to fail to live up to their potential to become loving people.

The fourth sin story is the Tower of Babel (Gen 11:1–9). Here, instead of filling the whole earth as God instructed them (Gen 1:28; 9:1), the people decide to settle down and make a name for themselves. They try to build a tower all the way to the heavens. Once more, sin prevails. Now the people are not only separated from God, but they are separated from each other. They don't even speak the same language. The stage has now been set for God to intervene in the course of human history and save God's people from their sinful choices. In Chapter 12 of Genesis, God calls Abram.

## MISTAKES IN INTERPRETATION

Now that we have put the story in context and seen what the inspired author is teaching, let us return to the claims made on behalf of the story by those who used it to defend slavery.

As we have said, neither the story of Noah nor the other three sin stories in the first eleven chapters of Genesis is claiming to be historical writing. The author has made that clear by the details in the story: an unrealistic plot and an anthropomorphic God. Therefore, one cannot make historical claims based on these stories, such as the claim that a historical Noah actually spoke Noah's curse. The story is not claiming that Noah was inspired by God to foresee future civilizations in which slavery would exist as part of God's plan, as the defenders of slavery claimed. Rather, the author was writing years after Israel had conquered Canaan and was using the literary device of foreshadowing. Through Noah's curse, he foreshadows Israel's conquering of Canaan after the exodus, something that was past history from the author's point of view.

An imaginative story that explains how something came to be as it is known to be from experience is called an *etiology*. Noah's curse is an etiology explaining how it is that the Israelites were able to conquer Canaan.

The passage says nothing at all about God's establishing slavery as a permanent part of the social order. To claim that it does is to take God's name in vain.

## THE HOLINESS CODE IN LEVITICUS

A second passage from the Old Testament used by slave owners to claim that slavery was part of God's social order is from the book of Leviticus: "As for the male and female slaves whom you may have, it is from the nations around you that you may acquire male and female slaves. You may also acquire them from among the aliens residing with you, and from their families that are with you, who have been born in your land; and they may be your property. You may keep them as a possession for your children after you, for them to inherit as property. These you may treat as slaves, but as for your fellow Israelites, no one shall rule over the other with harshness" (Lev 25:44–46).

Based on this passage, those who defended slavery claimed that God permitted the Israelites to purchase slaves who would be their property, to be handed down to their children as an inheritance. If owning slaves as inheritable property was moral for the Israelites, it was moral for the slave owners.[2]

What argument might a biblical contextualist offer a sincere slave owner to disabuse him of this conclusion? As always, we must consider context. In this instance, it is the context of the process of revelation that is being ignored.

As was explained in Chapter 1, the Bible models a two thousand-year process of coming to knowledge. Inspired authors had true insights on the topics they were addressing, but sometimes those insights were only part of the truth. It would take hundreds of years for later inspired authors to add to those partial truths.

The setting for this passage from Leviticus is the time of Moses (1250 BC). The time of the final editing of the account as we now have it is the same time as the story of Noah that we just discussed: after the Babylonian captivity (587–537 BC), when the Israelites had returned to the holy land, and the priests were retelling and editing their stories for the returned exiles.

The passage we are discussing is part of what is called the *holiness code* (Lev 17–26). The theme of the holiness code is: God is holy; God has chosen to dwell with us; we, too, must be holy. Over and over, God tells the Israelites, "Be holy, for I am holy" (Lev 19:2, 20, 26). The laws prescribed are instructions about how to be holy. These laws developed over time. However, in this account, they are "telescoped," that is, they are presented as having all been promulgated at the same time and all are attributed directly to God.

At the time of the setting of this story, the time of Moses, the Israelites understood that God loved them, but they did not yet understand that God loved everyone. So the way they treated their fellow Israelites was different from the way they treated other people, especially their enemies. This passage is a perfect example. The Israelites may have slaves, but they may not have fellow Israelites as slaves.

The holiness code teaches the Israelites to love their neighbors. God says: "You shall not take vengeance or bear a grudge against any of your people, but you shall love you neighbor as yourself: I am the Lord" (Lev 19:18). This instruction makes it clear that the Israelites were still in the process of understanding that God loves everyone. (So are we.) Their *neighbor* was understood to be their own people.

During and after the Babylonian exile, various inspired authors began to realize that God loves everyone, not just the Israelites. This is the theme of the book of Jonah, in which Jonah is told to go and preach to the Ninevites. Nineveh was the capital of Assyria, the country that conquered the ten northern tribes. Nineveh represented Israel's enemies. The author is teaching that God loves even the Israelites' enemies.

The New Testament illustrates that this same lack of understanding regarding the universal nature of God's love was present at the time of Jesus. This is obvious as we read the parable of the Good Samaritan as well as the conversation that precedes and follows it (Luke 10:25–37).

A lawyer asks Jesus what he must do to inherit eternal life. Jesus asks him: "What is written in the law? What do you read there" (Luke 10:26)? The lawyer gives a perfect answer, quoting both Deuteronomy 6:5 and Leviticus 19:18. He says, "You shall love the Lord your God with all your heart, and with all your soul, and with all your strength, and with all you mind; and your neighbor as yourself" (Luke 10:27). Obviously, the lawyer had asked a question to which he already knew the answer. He was trying to test Jesus, not learn from him. So, after giving a perfect answer to his own question, the lawyer wants to "justify" himself. He asks Jesus, "Who is my neighbor" (Luke 10:29)? Jesus then tells the parable of the Good Samaritan, holding up as neighbor the very person the lawyer would, by law, not consider a neighbor: the unclean Samaritan.

Jesus was teaching the lawyer, his contemporaries, and us that we need to broaden our understanding of *neighbor*. If God created everyone, God loves everyone. All other human beings are not only our neighbors, but our brothers and sisters. Scripture does not limit our understanding of whom we are to love to the understanding of the chosen people in 1250 BC, or even to the understanding of Jesus's contemporaries. It is in the Acts of the Apostles that we learn that God's covenant, God's love and promise of fidelity, are offered to every human being, not just to one chosen group (Acts 10:34–36). The good news is that all are loved. All are chosen. If we live in fidelity to the commandment "Love your neighbor," we will not claim to own our neighbor, treating our neighbor as property.

Had the slave owners put Leviticus 25:44–46 in the context of a two thousand year process of coming to knowledge, they would not have used the passage to justify slavery in the United States in the nineteenth century. They would not have taken God's name in vain.

## THE NEW TESTAMENT AND SLAVERY

Another argument used by slaveholders to defend the morality of slavery is that the New Testament supports the institution of slavery. Jesus never preached against it. Paul returned the slave Onesimus to his owner, Philemon (see Phil 12); Paul directed slaves who became Christian to remain as slaves (see 1 Cor 7:21–24); and letter after letter contains specific instructions to slaves that they should be obedient to their masters.[3] The following passages were all used to support slavery as being moral:

> Slaves, obey your earthly masters with fear and trembling, in singleness of heart, as you obey Christ; not only while being watched, and in order to please them, but as slaves of Christ, doing the will of God from the heart. Render service with enthusiasm, as to the Lord and not to men and women, knowing that whatever good we do, we will receive the same again from the Lord, whether we are slaves or free. (Eph 6:5–8)

> Slaves, obey your earthly masters in everything, not only while being watched and in order to please them, but wholeheartedly, fearing the Lord. Whatever your task, put yourselves into it, as done for the Lord and not for your masters, since you know that from the Lord you will receive the inheritance as your reward; you serve the Lord Christ. (Col 3:22–24)

> Let all who are under the yoke of slavery regard their masters as worthy of all honor, so that the name of God and the teaching may not be blasphemed. Those who have believing masters must not be disrespectful to them on the

ground that they are members of the church; rather they must serve them all the more, since those who benefit by their service are believers and beloved. (1 Tim 6:1–2)

Tell slaves to be submissive to their masters and to give satisfaction in every respect; they are not to talk back, not to pilfer, but to show complete and perfect fidelity, so that in everything they may be an ornament to the doctrine of God our Savior. (Titus 2:8–10)

Slaves, accept the authority of your masters with all deference, not only those who are kind and gentle but also those who are harsh. For it is a credit to you if, being aware of God, you endure pain while suffering unjustly. (1 Peter 2:18–19)

Given these passages, how can one possibly argue that slavery is immoral?

We discussed this topic briefly in Chapter 1, using the passage from Ephesians that directs slaves to obey their masters as an example of the necessity to consider the context of the presumptions of the time of the author and audience. What all of these passages demonstrate is that slavery was a given in the Roman Empire. Slavery was part of the fabric of society. The authors of the letters did not ask if slavery should be part of the social order. It was. They simply applied the core truth, that Christians were to treat every other person as though that person were Christ, to the society in which their audience lived.

In Ephesians, the directions are not just to slaves. They are also to masters. Masters are to remember that they, too, have a master in heaven, and they are accountable to that master for the way in which they treat those over whom they have authority: "And master, do the same to them. Stop threatening them, for you know that both of you have the same Master in heaven, and with him there is no partiality" (Eph 5:9). To apply the core truth to the masters as well as to the slaves was a bold and revolutionary thing to do.

Paul understood and taught that with Christ all social distinctions become spiritually insignificant. Paul says, ". . . for in Christ Jesus you are all children of God through faith. As many of you as were baptized into Christ have clothed yourselves with Christ. There is no longer Jew or Greek, there is no longer slave or free, there is no longer male and female; for all of you are one in Christ Jesus" (Gal 3:26–29a).

In addition, Paul wanted the slave owner Philemon not to punish his slave Onesimus for leaving, and even wanted Philemon to set Onesimus free. Paul says: "I am appealing to you for my child, Onesimus, whose father I have become during my imprisonment. I am sending him, that is, my own heart, back to you. I wanted to keep him with me, so that he might be of service to me in your place during my imprisonment for the gospel; but I preferred to do nothing without your consent, in order that your good deed might be voluntary and not something forced" (Phil 10–14). In other words, Paul realized that Philemon owned Onesimus, but he wanted Philemon to freely give up his property rights and set Onesimus free.

Christians were a minority group. As we will see once more when we discuss the role of women in the Church, Christians were not encouraged to act in ways that would result in persecution, such as violating another person's property rights. However, Christians were taught about their own dignity and the dignity of every other person. They were also taught to treat others with the dignity they deserved as beloved children of God. This core truth, the dignity of each person, applied to various social orders, inevitably led Christians to the conclusion that slavery was immoral.

We see, then, that if the Christians who used the Bible to support slavery had known how to put Scripture passages in context, they may not have unwittingly abused the Bible, thus putting God's authority behind their own misunderstandings. An understanding of literary form would have prevented them from making historical claims about Noah's curse. An understanding that Scripture models a two thousand-year process of revelation would have enabled them to understand Leviticus as an early step in that process, not the fullness of understanding, on the topic of love of neighbor. An understanding of the presumptions of the time, the "givens" between author and audience would have prepared slave owners to understand that the letters were written to people who lived in a social order in which the ownership of both slaves and wives was accepted. The authors simply accepted the social order as it existed and applied Christ's message of love to that social order.

Knowledge of these three contexts will be just as helpful to us, today, as we examine social issues and turn to Scripture to help us discern right from wrong. After all, we don't want to claim, "The Bible tells me so," unless the Bible actually does tell us so.

## NOTES

1. For a full discussion of this argument and examples of such claims, see Larry R. Morrison, "The Religious Defense of American Slavery Before 1830," *Journal of Religious Thought* (Washington, DC: Howard University School of Divinity, 1980), 17–18.

2. Morrison, 18–19.

3. Morrison, 19, 24–27.

## Chapter Three

# Women Should Not Vote:
# Their Place Is in the Home

*Does the Bible Tell Me So?*
*No*

In our last chapter, we saw how Scripture was used to support slavery as it was practiced in the United States: Noah's curse was used to claim that God established the social order that included slavery. Various New Testament passages were used to affirm this order. In every instance, the people using Scripture to support slavery were ignoring context.

Scripture was also used to argue against women being allowed to vote. Once again, a "curse" in the book of Genesis, Eve's curse, was used to support the belief that God established the social order in which women were inferior and, therefore, subordinate. Once again, various New Testament passages were used to affirm this social order. In this chapter, we will look at the ways in which Scripture was used to deny women the vote in the United States, and then examine what mistakes in interpretation led to this abuse of Scripture.

On the question of slavery, I expressed the opinion that, as a nation, we have come to agreement on the subject. On the question of women's right to vote, I think we have also come to agreement. However, on the question of women's rights across a spectrum of other issues, we have not yet come to agreement. Therefore, some readers may feel more resistant to my saying that Scripture was abused when it was used to support the anti-suffrage movement than they did when I said that Scripture was abused when it was used to support slavery. Deeply rooted cultural convictions that have been "proof texted" from the Bible by people whom we trust and admire are hard to outgrow because we hold them as religious convictions. Nevertheless, Scripture calls us to grow in love. The more we grow in love, the more we realize that we are taking God's name in vain when we use Scripture to argue for a social order that subordinates whole groups of people, such as African Americans or women.

## THE CLAIM: GOD CREATED
## WOMEN TO SERVE MEN

Those who fought against women's suffrage often did so based on religious claims. They believed, based on the story of Adam and Eve in Genesis, that women were created for men and that a woman's role was simply to obey her husband. After all, in Genesis God says, "It is not good that the man should be alone; I will make him a helper as his partner" (Gen 2:18). Therefore, women were created to be men's helpers. In addition, after the man and woman ate from the forbidden tree, God told the woman, ". . . your desire will be for your husband, and he shall rule over you" (Gen 3:16b). So it is part of God's law that men have authority over women. For women to vote, thus assuming a role in public affairs rather than domestic affairs, was to violate God's created order.[1]

As was true with the use of Noah's curse to support slavery, the use of the story of Adam and Eve to argue against women's suffrage is an abuse of Scripture. Those who used Scripture in this way failed to consider context. They failed to ask if the inspired author of the story of the man and woman in the garden was addressing the same question that they were using the passage to address. In particular, they failed to consider literary form.

## LITERARY FORM

As was stated earlier, the story of Adam and Eve does not present itself as historical writing. This is evident from the way the author tells the story. First, the author uses personification: a major character in the story is a talking snake. In addition, the author presents us with an anthropomorphic picture of God: God realizes that it is not good for the man to be alone, but God's first attempts to provide man with a helper don't work out: ". . . but for the man there was not found a helper as his partner" (Gen 2:21). This anthropomorphic God is not all knowing. After the man and woman eat from the forbidden tree, God comes for God's usual evening walk and talk. God is pictured as not realizing that anything is wrong until the man and woman hide. After Adam explains that he is hiding because he is naked, God says, "Who told you that you were naked? Have you eaten from the tree of which I commanded you not to eat" (Gen 3:11)?

Still more evidence that the author is not writing history is the author's use of symbols. Despite the depiction of many artists, the tree in the garden is not an apple tree, but a *tree of the knowledge of good and evil*. The garden also has a *tree of life*. These trees are symbols, not descriptions of actual trees. Since we are reading an imaginative and symbolic story, we cannot use the account to make historical claims. We cannot claim that Adam and Eve are historical people or that, in response to their sin, God established a social order in which men would always lord it over their wives.

## WHAT IS THE STORY TEACHING?

The author of the story of Adam and Eve is not responding to the question "What role should women have in society?" but to the question "Why do human beings suffer?" To probe this mystery, the author pictures a garden in which God places a person. That person is called *Adam*. *Adam* is a neuter, collective noun, not a masculine, singular noun. So *Adam*, too, is a symbol. Adam is each of us and all of us. As the story begins, the man and woman are not suffering because all of their relationships are in right order: their relationship with self, their relationship with each other, their relationship with God, and their relationship with the earth. God's telling the man and woman not to eat of the tree of knowledge of good and evil symbolizes the fact that there is a moral order, a moral order that has been revealed. There is right, and there is wrong.

After the man and woman disobey God's order, that is, after they choose to sin, all of their relationships are broken. The man and woman hide from God, Adam blames Eve for his action, they are now ashamed of their nakedness, and their relationship with the earth is disrupted. Suffering is now part of their experience.

In answer to the question "Why do human beings suffer?" the author is teaching that suffering is the consequence of sin. The author pictures God explaining the kinds of suffering that are common to the human race, sufferings that the author knows exist from experience. One example of this suffering is that the man will rule over the woman. This author is not picturing God establishing God's order for society. Rather, the author is picturing God explaining the disorder that has been caused by sin. As we learned in the first story in Genesis, man and woman were both made in God's own image; both are of ultimate and equal dignity (Gen 1:27). Now God's order has been destroyed by sin. To use Eve's curse (Gen 3:16) to claim that God's social order denies women a voice in public affairs is to abuse Scripture and to take God's name in vain.

## THE NEW TESTAMENT AND WOMEN'S ROLE

As was true in the debates over slavery, many New Testament passages were used to argue against women having the right to vote. In every case, those who abused Scripture failed to consider context when determining what the inspired authors were teaching.

For instance, a passage in 1 Corinthians that alludes to the Genesis story that we just discussed says, "But I want you to understand that Christ is the head of every man, and the husband is the head of his wife, and God is the head of Christ . . . since [man] is the image and reflection of God; but woman is the reflection of man. . . . Indeed, man was not made from woman, but woman from man. Neither was man created for the sake of woman, but woman for the sake of man . . . " (1 Cor 11:3, 7, 9).

To put this passage in context, we must first ask in what literary form the passage appears. 1 Corinthians is a letter, a literary form with which we are very familiar. When we write a letter, we speak to a particular audience and address issues in the context of that relationship. Paul knows the Corinthians well. He established the Church in Corinth (see Acts 18:1–28). Now, Paul is writing the Corinthians, responding to some questions that they have asked and to some reports that he has received about them (see 1 Cor 1:11; 11:18).

The question that Paul is addressing is not whether women should have a role in public affairs, whether women should be allowed to vote. In fact, it is not even about whether women should have a role in public worship, in a church service. Paul is assuming that women will have leadership roles. The argument is over how women should dress when they pray or prophesy in church.

Paul feels strongly that neither men nor women should draw attention to themselves by violating social customs at worship. Men should look like men: they should have short hair and not cover their heads. Women should look like women: they should have long hair and keep it covered. "Any man who prays or prophesies with something on his head disgraces his head, but any woman who prays or prophesies with her head unveiled disgraces her head . . . " (1 Cor 11:4–5).

When Paul refers to man being woman's "head," he is not claiming that man is woman's boss, but that man is woman's source. He is alluding to the Adam and Eve story. In that story, Eve is made from Adam's rib, so he is her source. We use the word "head" in the same way when we refer to the head of a river. We are referring to the river's source. Paul says that God is the head of Christ because God is Christ's source.

Paul is not claiming that men are superior to women, just that they are different, and that difference should be apparent in their dress. To assure that his words are not misinterpreted, Paul says: "Nevertheless, in the Lord woman is not independent of man or man independent of woman. For just as woman came from man, so man comes through woman; but all things come from God" (1 Cor 11:11–12). As he winds down his argument, Paul acknowledges that this subject deals simply with local social customs: "But if anyone is disposed to be contentious—we have no such custom, nor do the churches of God" (1 Cor 11:16).

Another passage quoted by those against women's suffrage also appears in 1 Corinthians: ". . . women should be silent in the churches. For they are not permitted to speak, but should be subordinate, as the law also says. If there is anything they desire to know, let them ask their husbands at home. For it is shameful for a woman to speak in church" (1 Cor 14:34–35).

This passage is particularly puzzling because it appears to directly contradict the earlier passage that directs women as well as men to dress properly when they fulfill public roles in church. A similar passage appears in 1 Timothy: "Let a woman learn in silence with full submission. I permit no woman to teach or to have authority over a man; she is to keep silent. For Adam was formed first, then Eve; and Adam was not deceived, but the woman was deceived and became a transgressor. Yet she will be saved through childbearing, provided they continue in faith and love and holiness, with modesty" (1 Tim 2:11–15).

These passages demand an explanation, especially since, when taken out of their social context, they appear to deny women roles in the church that they had previously fulfilled, roles such as leading prayer and prophesying. Scripture scholars surmise that the passages from 1 Corinthians and 1 Timothy that limit women's roles are from a later date than the passage from 1 Corinthians 11 that instructs women on proper dress. In the very early church, women did have leadership roles in home churches. However, such roles were a challenge to Roman society and women's roles in the Roman Empire at that time. Church leaders began to advise against challenging Roman society in this way in order to avoid persecution.

Additional evidence that 1 Corinthians 14:34–35 did not originate with Paul is that the author appeals to the law for his authority: "[Women] should be subordinate, as the law also says" (1 Cor 14:34). Central to Paul's understanding of the good news of Jesus Christ is that salvation comes through faith, not through obedience to the law. Scripture scholars think it unlikely that Paul would have turned to the law to add authority to his teaching.

Thus, none of these passages can be accurately used to prove that women should not have a voice in public affairs, that women should not vote. If we applied these passages to today's setting, we could fairly say that both women and men should dress in a way appropriate to the culture when they have public roles in worship, and that it is wise not to act in ways that attract persecution.

Still another New Testament passage used against women's suffrage is from Ephesians: "Wives, be subject to your husbands as you are to the Lord.

For the husband is the head of the wife just as Christ is the head of the church, the body of which he is the Savior. Just as the church is subject to Christ, so also wives ought to be subject, in everything, to their husbands" (Eph 5:22–24).

This passage is parallel to the "Slaves be obedient to your masters" passage that we discussed in Chapters 1 and 2. The admonition to wives to be subject to their husbands is an application of a core truth to a particular social setting, not the core truth itself. The core truth is "Therefore be imitators of God, as beloved children, and live in love, as Christ loved us and gave himself up for us . . . " (Eph 5:1–2).

Paul is helping the Ephesians apply this insight to the social situation in which they live. In that setting, slaves and wives were property. Men could have treated their wives and slaves cruelly if they chose to do so. Paul admonishes men with authority to remember that they also are accountable to authority: they are accountable to God, and they will be held responsible for their actions (Eph 6:9). Husbands and masters must act with love toward those over whom they have authority.

At the same time, slaves, wives, and children, all of whom are under authority, should treat the person in authority with respect. They should treat their masters, husbands, and fathers as they would Christ. Paul does say: "Just as the church is subject to Christ, so also wives ought to be, in everything, subject to their husbands" (Eph 5:24). However, that statement is in the context of an earlier statement, addressed to everyone in the household: "Be subject to one another out of reverence for Christ" (Eph 5:21).

What are we to learn from this passage? The core truth is that we must treat every other person as we would treat Christ. However, we must apply that core truth to our own social setting and discern just how we should act to be faithful to that core truth. We must not put the authority of Scripture behind Paul's applying the core truth to a social setting in which wives and slaves were property.

## WHAT IS THE LOVING THING TO DO?

Some readers who still believe that it is God's order that wives be subject to their husbands in all things, rather than that husbands and wives should be subject to each other, will feel resistant to the explanations just given. They may well say, "You don't really respect the authority of the Bible. You simply pick and choose, accepting only those passages with which you agree." Perhaps an example of applying the core truth (that we must act lovingly) to a question in which we have no vested interest will make the importance of this distinction between core truth and application to a particular social setting more persuasive.

A question of great importance to first-century Christians was: May we eat meat that has been sacrificed to an idol, or not? In the Roman Empire, many gods were worshipped by many different people. After sacrificing animals to gods, people would sell the sacrificed meat in the meat markets. Would it be permissible for a Christian to buy and eat this meat, or would eating the meat be tantamount to honoring that other god, in some sense joining oneself to the sacrifice that was made in that god's honor?

Paul's first letter to the Corinthians and the book of Revelation give different answers to this question, not because they disagree on the issue, but because they are applying the core truth, love your neighbor, to different social settings. Paul is applying the core truth to a setting in which the people are not experiencing persecution. The author of Revelations is applying the core truth to a setting in which there is persecution.

Paul tells the Corinthians that it is permissible to eat meat that has been sacrificed to idols as long as, in doing so, they do not scandalize and harm the conscience of a person who does not understand why a Christian could do this in good conscience. Paul's reasoning is that there is only one God, the God whom Jews and Christians worship. Therefore, even though someone had the intent of offering food to another god, the food was not actually offered to another god because there is no other God. Therefore, Christians do not sin when they eat food that has been sacrificed to an idol. Paul says, "We are no worse off if we do not eat, and no better off if we do" (1 Cor 8:8).

However, Christians are not to exercise this freedom if doing so would hurt another. Paul says, "It is not everyone, however, who has this knowledge. Since some have become so accustomed to idols until now, they still think of the food they eat as food offered to an idol; and their conscience, being weak, is defiled" (1 Cor 8:7). Paul concludes that, in such a case, it would be a sin to eat meat sacrificed to an idol. Paul goes on to say: "But when you thus sin against members of your family, and wound their conscience when it is weak, you sin against Christ" (1 Cor 8:12).

So Paul's answer is that the morality of the action depends on the social setting. In some settings, one action is more loving than another.

However, if we did not have Paul's first letter to the Corinthians, but had only the book of Revelation, we would have a clear condemnation of eating food sacrificed to idols: no ifs, ands, or buts. The author of Revelation is writing to particular communities who are facing persecution. In two of the opening letters, the letters to Pergamum and Thyatira, the author condemns the people for having eaten food sacrificed to idols.

To the Pergamums the author says: "But I have a few things against you: you have some there who hold to the teaching of Balaam, who taught Balak to put a stumbling block before the people of Israel so that they would eat food sacrificed to idols and practice fornication" (Rev 2:14). To the Thyatirans he says: "But I have this against you: you tolerate that woman Jezebel, who calls herself a prophet and is teaching and beguiling my servant to practice fornication and to eat food sacrificed to idols" (Rev 2:20).

The book of Revelation is written in a literary form called *apocalyptic literature*. Apocalyptic literature is a kind of writing in code to persecuted people to offer them hope that their sufferings would soon end and to encourage them to remain faithful in the meantime. The setting of persecution is presumed known between the author and the audience. Given that setting, to eat meat sacrificed to idols could well give others the impression that one is choosing infidelity over persecution, placating the Roman persecutors. To do so would not be a loving action, and Revelation condemns it, considering it just as wrong as another kind of infidelity, fornication.

So what Paul says about how members of a household should treat one another when he is addressing his words to a culture in which slaves and wives are property is not necessarily what he would say about household behavior in a culture in which the dignity of every person, as a person responsible to God, is recognized. In neither case would Paul be teaching the social order. The social order is a given. Rather, Paul is teaching the Gospel, the good news of Jesus Christ. That good news is that Christ loves each person. So, the way we treat every other person is the way we are treating the risen Christ. It is that truth that must be applied to every social order.

Once that truth is applied to a social order, the social order often changes, as happened in the United States. Masters realized that they shouldn't consider other people as their property. Husbands realized that they shouldn't lord it over their wives. Slowly, the great dignity of each person, made in the image of God, was more clearly understood.

We see, then, that to use Scripture to proof text that women should not have a voice in public affairs and should not be able to vote was an abuse of Scripture. It rested on a cultural presumption that women are inferior to men, not only weaker physically, but less intelligent.

Although we are still involved in the process, I think that, in many ways, people in the United States have outgrown this cultural presumption. It is mind boggling to many people who are alive today to realize that women in the United States were denied the vote until so recently. It was not until 1920 that the 19th Amendment to the Constitution affirmed that the right of a citizen to vote could not be abridged by the United States or the states based on sex. Even after women's right to vote was secured, black women were often unable to vote because of literacy tests and poll taxes aimed at excluding them. The right of all citizens to vote, whether white or black, male or female, was not secured until the Voting Rights Acts of 1965.

Given the arguments used against women's suffrage, it is very evident that the tendency to abuse Scripture to support what one already thinks was alive and well in the twentieth century. The question is: Is it still alive and well in the twenty-first century? Are we still claiming, "The Bible tells me so," when the Bible says no such thing?

## NOTE

1. To read examples of such claims, see "The Bible and Gender Equality." http://www.stopthereligious right.org/suffrage.htm (accessed March 25, 2014).

*Chapter Four*

# Jesus Loves Me

*Does the Bible Tell Me So?*
*Yes*

In demonstrating how Scripture was abused to support slavery and to oppose women's suffrage, we claimed that, in his letters, Paul was teaching the good news of the Gospel, not about the social order of his time. What is that good news? An all-important part of the good news is that God loves every person and invites every person into an intimate relationship of love. This good news was revealed by Jesus Christ, who dwelt among us, taught us, endured death on a cross for us, rose from the dead, and remains in our midst. Jesus invites us to follow him.

Those who accept the authority of the New Testament agree with these claims. However, many who quote Scripture, claiming that it adds authority to their preconceptions and prejudices, fail to understand the ramifications of the Gospel's good news: They understand the truth of the words, "Jesus loves *me*," when the words are on *their* lips, but they seem not to understand the ramifications of the words in relation to others. They feel right with God, justified, even while they are judging and excluding others.

It seems that among those who find it difficult to accept the good news are those who, for some reason or other (be it gender, social status, education, wealth, race, etc.), feel a sense of superiority, a sense of being better than others, a sense, not only of being chosen, but of being chosen over others.

We have already discussed several examples of this kind of behavior: Those who supported slavery believed that whites were superior to blacks. Those who objected to women's suffrage believed that men were intellectually superior to women. They then tried to use Scripture to support their sense of superiority as God's own order.

Jesus met many people whose sense of superiority caused them to be self-righteous and judgmental. As a result, they rejected Jesus and his good news. They failed to accept the invitation that Jesus continued to offer them.

In this chapter, we will examine the ramifications of being loved by Jesus Christ. As we will see, the good news challenges us in many, many ways: in our sense of being more loved by God than others, in our inclination to judge others as less worthy than ourselves, in our reluctance to forgive others, in our inclination to accumulate material goods to the detriment of others, and in our sense of responsibility, or lack of responsibility, for others. The good news of the Gospel requires us to act lovingly toward all. Whenever we judge and exclude others, rather than love them, we are failing to live up to the Gospel. When we use Scripture to support our actions we are truly taking God's name in vain.

## WHO IS MY NEIGHBOR?

Many religious people have, as part of their religious conviction, strong prejudices against other people. Perhaps their prejudice is against those of another nationality or another race. Perhaps it is against those of different social strata. Perhaps it is against those of another sexual orientation. Perhaps it is against those of another religion. Whatever it is, they feel religiously justified to judge and exclude those people.

As we discussed briefly in Chapter 2, we read about Jesus meeting just such a person in Luke's Gospel (see Luke 10:25–37). The lawyer who first asked Jesus, "What must I do to inherit eternal life?" (Luke 10:25b) and then asked, "Who is my neighbor?" (Luke 10:29b), felt completely justified in failing to love Samaritans. Samaritans were considered unclean by the Jews, so the Jews did not share things in common with them (see John 4:9). In response to the lawyer's question, "Who is my neighbor?" Jesus tells him the Good Samaritan story.

A man (we are not told his nationality) was accosted by robbers and left in a ditch. A priest and a Levite, both leaders in the Jewish community whom the lawyer would consider to be neighbors, saw the man in the ditch, but passed him by. However, a Samaritan, whom the lawyer would not consider to be a neighbor, saw the man and took care of him. After telling this story, Jesus asks the lawyer, "Which of these three, do you think, was a neighbor to the man who fell into the hands of the robbers" (Luke 10:36)?

The lawyer obviously understands the significance of Jesus's parable, but he can't bring himself to say that the Samaritan acted as a neighbor. So instead he says, "The one who showed him mercy" (Luke 10:37a). Jesus tells the lawyer to "go and do likewise" (Luke 10:37b). Through the parable of the Good Samaritan, Jesus is teaching the lawyer that the Samaritan, too, is the lawyer's neighbor. The lawyer must learn to love even the Samaritan in order to inherit eternal life.

If Jesus were to tell this story to a self-righteous Christian today, who would be the one who acted as neighbor in the story? Would it be an undocumented immigrant? Would it be a person of another world religion? Would it be a convicted felon? Whoever it would be, the point of the story would be to gently invite the self-righteous questioner to learn to include that group in his or her understanding of a neighbor who must be loved.

## WHO IS A SINNER?

It is interesting to note that Jesus's call to repentance and his invitation to the kingdom were more readily accepted by people who acknowledged that they were sinners than by people who felt superior to those whom they regarded as sinners.

Jesus taught this truth to "some who trusted in themselves that they were righteous and regarded others with contempt" (Luke 18:9) when he told them the parable of the two men who went to the temple to pray (see Luke 18:9–14). One man was a Pharisee; the other was a tax collector. "The Pharisee, standing by himself, was praying thus, 'God I thank you that I am not like other people; thieves, rogues, adulterers, or even like this tax collector'" (Luke 18:11). The Pharisee then goes on to brag to God that he fasts twice a week and tithes.

The tax collector prays in an entirely different manner. He says, "God, be merciful to me, a sinner" (Luke 18:13b)! Jesus then comments that "this man went down to his home justified rather than the other; for all who exalt themselves will be humbled, but all who humble themselves will be exalted" (Luke 18:14).

Another example of a sinner who realizes that he is a sinner and so repents is Zacchaeus, a rich tax collector (see Luke 19:1–10). Tax collectors were universally looked down upon because they were working for the Roman occupiers of the holy land. A rich tax collector was the worst of the worst, a person who collected more taxes than were required in order to enrich himself.

Jesus sought out sinners. So Jesus invited himself to Zacchaeus's house. Those watching said, "He has gone to be the guest of one who is a sinner" (Luke 19:7b). This is a true statement. However, it would be a true statement no matter in whose home Jesus chose to dine. Those who complained evidently didn't realize that they, too, were sinners.

In contrast, Zacchaeus did realize that he was a sinner, and he repented. Zacchaeus says: "Look, half of my possessions, Lord, I will give to the poor; and if I have defrauded anyone of anything, I will pay back four times as much" (Luke 19:8). Jesus tells Zacchaeus, "Today salvation has come to this house" (Luke 19:9a).

Jesus offered his gift of salvation to everyone. However, not everyone accepted Jesus or the truth of what he was teaching. It seems that the hardest people for Jesus to reach were those who did not realize that they, too, were sinners. They could see sin in others, but not in themselves. It was to people like this that Jesus told the parable of the prodigal son.

Luke tells us that tax collectors and sinners were coming to listen to Jesus. However, "the Pharisees and the scribes were grumbling and saying, 'This fellow welcomes sinners and eats with them'" (Luke 15:2). In response to this criticism, Jesus tells the Pharisees and scribes three stories: the parable of the lost sheep (Luke 15:3–7), the parable of the lost coin (Luke 15:8–10), and the parable of the prodigal son (Luke 15:11–32). The first two parables are teaching Jesus's critics that it is perfectly normal to seek out that which one has lost and to rejoice when it is found. Any of them would do the same. However, in the parable of the prodigal son, Jesus tries to teach his self-righteous judges that they themselves are sinners because they fail to love their fellow sinners.

In the story that Jesus tells his critics, a father has two sons. The older son is completely obedient, reliable, and respectful; the younger son is anything but obedient, reliable, and respectful. The younger son asks his father for his inheritance, wastes it in a sinful lifestyle, and ends up feeding pigs just to support himself. Think what shame would be involved for a Jewish person who considered eating pork abhorrent (see Deut 14:3–8) to find himself reduced to feeding pigs!

Realizing that the pigs are eating better than he is, and that his father's servants are not suffering from hunger, he decides to return home, acknowledge his unworthiness, and ask to be accepted back as a hired hand. When he returns, his father sees him coming from a distance. His father "ran and put his arms around him and kissed him" (Luke 15:20b). The father is so joyful at his lost son's return that he tells the servants: "Quickly, bring out a robe—the best one—and put it on him; put a ring on his finger and sandals on his feet. And get the fatted calf and kill it, and let us eat and celebrate; for this son of mine was dead and is alive again; he was lost and is found" (Luke 15:22–24)!

Enter the older, obedient, reliable son. Coming back from the field and realizing that some sort of celebration is occurring, he hears from a servant that the celebration is in honor of his younger brother, who has suddenly returned. He becomes very angry and refuses to join the party.

The father loves both sons. Just as he went out and greeted his younger son, he goes out and tries to reassure his older son. The older son says: "Listen! For all these years I have been working like a slave for you, and I have never disobeyed your command; yet you have never given me even a young goat so that I might celebrate with my friends. But when this son of yours came back, who has devoured your property with prostitutes, you killed the fatted calf for him" (Luke 15:29–30)!

The Pharisees and scribes to whom Jesus is telling the story are just like this older son. They have obeyed the law, and they feel superior to sinners who have failed to obey the law. They are fully aware of the sins of others, but completely unaware of their own sins, their own inability to forgive, welcome back, and love, other sinners.

The father in the story tells his older son what Jesus is telling his critics: "Son, you are always with me, and all that is mine is yours. But we had to celebrate and rejoice, because this brother of yours was dead and has come to life; he was lost and has been found" (Luke 15:31–32).

The story ends before we know whether the older brother relents, forgives, and joins the celebration. In ending the story there, Jesus is challenging the Pharisees and scribes, who are acting like the older brother, to decide whether they will accept Jesus's invitation into the kingdom. They are definitely invited. They are definitely forgiven. The question is whether they will realize that they, too, are sinners and will respond to Jesus's plea to repent because the kingdom of God is at hand.

## WHOM MUST I FORGIVE?

In Jesus's parable of the prodigal son, the older brother did not realize that in order to be in right relationship with his father he must find it in his heart to forgive his younger brother. Through the parable, Jesus was teaching the Pharisees and scribes that in order to be in right relationship with God, they must learn to forgive sinners. The good news of the Gospel requires the same thing of those who realize that "Jesus loves me." To accept Jesus's invitation to the kingdom, we must repent of our sins, including the sins of feeling superior to anyone, excluding anyone, or failing to forgive anyone. Disciples of Jesus Christ must always be willing to forgive.

This truth is taught over and over in the Gospels. In Matthew's Gospel, Peter asks Jesus, "'Lord, if another member of the church sins against me, how often should I forgive: As many as seven times?' Jesus said to him, 'Not seven times, but, I tell you, seventy-seven times'" (Matt 18:21–22). Obviously, Jesus is not teaching Peter that he should keep a log and stop forgiving someone after seventy-seven times. Peter is to forgive always.

Jesus then tells a parable in which a servant who is forgiven a debt to his master refuses to forgive a person in debt to him (Matt 18:23–35). On hearing of this, the master "handed him over to be tortured until he would pay his entire debt" (Matt 18:34). Jesus is teaching Peter and the other disciples that they are like the forgiven servant. Just as they have been forgiven, so must they forgive others.

Jesus had earlier taught the disciples the same relationship between having been forgiven and forgiving others when he taught them how to pray. Jesus says: "Pray then in this way: Our Father in heaven, / hallowed be your name. . . . And forgive us our debts, / as we also have forgiven our debtors . . . " (Matt 6:9, 12). It is a sobering thought to realize that when we say this prayer, we are asking God to forgive us only to the extent that we have forgiven others.

In his Gospel, Luke teaches the necessity of forgiveness even in the most difficult circumstances by picturing Jesus forgiving those who crucified him while the crucifixion was taking place. Jesus says, "Father, forgive them; for they do not know what they are doing" (Luke 23:34). Jesus also forgives one of the criminals crucified with him saying, "Truly I tell you, today you will be with me in Paradise" (Luke 29:43). Luke continues this theme when he pictures Jesus commissioning the disciples. Jesus says, "Thus it is written that the Messiah is to suffer and to rise from the dead on the third day, and that repentance and forgiveness of sins is to be proclaimed in his name to all nations, beginning from Jerusalem" (Luke 24:46–47).

We see, then, that we cannot fail to forgive others and be in right relationship with God ourselves. It is not that we earn God's forgiveness by forgiving others. We do not earn God's love or forgiveness. It is a grace, an unearned gift. Rather, we fail to accept the gift that has been offered when we refuse to forgive others. Like the self-righteous Pharisees and scribes, we don't even realize that we have sinned. Therefore, we fail to repent, and we exclude ourselves from the invitation to the kingdom of God.

Luke pictures Jesus teaching this lesson to a Pharisee who has invited Jesus to dinner (see Luke 7:36–50). A woman, a known sinner, comes in and starts to wash Jesus's feet. The Pharisee says to himself, "If this man were a prophet, he would have known who and what kind of woman this is who is touching him—that she is a sinner" (Luke 7:39b). Jesus knows what the man is thinking and so tells him the parable of the two debtors.

In the parable, a creditor forgives one debtor a debt of 500 denarii and the other a debt of fifty denarii. Jesus asks the Pharisee, "Now which of them will love him more" (Luke 7:42b)? The Pharisee responds, "I suppose the one for whom he canceled the greater debt" (Luke 7:43a). Jesus then compares the woman whom the Pharisee would judge and exclude to the debtor who has been forgiven much, and the Pharisee to the debtor who has been forgiven little.

The woman loves more than the Pharisee does because she knows she has been forgiven much. She did not earn forgiveness because she loved. She experienced forgiveness and responded with love. Jesus says, "I tell you, her sins, which were many, have been forgiven; hence she has shown great love" (Luke 7:47a).

Jesus loves both the Pharisee and the woman. Jesus is not socializing with the Pharisee because it is an honor to be in the Pharisee's company. He is dining with the Pharisee because Jesus seeks out the lost. Jesus is trying to teach the Pharisee truths to which his self-righteous, judgmental, and unforgiving actions have made him blind. The Pharisee doesn't realize this, but when Jesus is dining with him, Jesus is dining with a sinner.

When we embrace the profound truth that "Jesus loves me," and we live in that love, we come, sometimes slowly, to the realization that Jesus also loves everyone: literally everyone. A disciple of Jesus Christ is called to be a witness of that love to others. We cannot "love much" until we realize that we, too, have been forgiven much. Once we realize that we have been forgiven much, we become more loving. We become more willing to forgive others.

## ISN'T WEALTH A GIFT FROM GOD?

Another truth that Jesus taught those whom he loved is that the accumulation of wealth should not be his followers' goal. There are several reasons for this. One is that wealthy people are tempted to put their trust in their own wealth rather than to put their trust in God's provident care, thus missing the experience and the resulting gratitude of knowing that God is with them and is providing for them.

This is why Jesus tells his disciples not to worry about their food or their clothes: "Look at the birds of the air; they neither sow nor reap nor gather into barns, and yet your heavenly Father feeds them. Are you not of more value than they? . . . But if God so clothes the grass of the field, which is alive today and tomorrow is thrown into the oven, will he not much more clothe you—you of little faith? . . . Strive first for the kingdom of God and his righteousness, and all these things will be given to you as well" (Matt 6:26, 30, 33).

It is because they should put their faith in God's provident care that Jesus instructs his disciples to travel light on their missionary journeys: "Take no gold, or silver, or copper in your belts, no bag for your journey, or two tunics, or sandals, or a staff . . . " (Matt 10:9–10). Rather than trusting in their own devices, they should rely on God and accept the hospitality of those whom they serve.

Another reason why wealth should not be a goal is that people will begin to love their wealth and make choices in order to keep it, rather than to follow Christ. An example of this is the rich young man (see Matt 19:16–22). This young man wanted to know what he must do to have eternal life. Jesus tells him that he must obey the commandments. The young man said, "'I have kept all these; what do I still lack?' Jesus said to him, 'If you wish to be perfect, go, sell your possessions, and give the money to the poor, and you will have treasure in heaven; then come follow me.' When the young man heard this word, he went away grieving, for he had many possessions" (Matt 19:20–22). The rich man wanted to remain rich more than he wanted to follow Christ.

Jesus then remarks to the disciples that it is very difficult to have wealth and not to begin to desire wealth more than to desire the kingdom of God: "Truly I tell you, it will be hard for a rich person to enter the kingdom of heaven. Again I tell you, it is easier for a camel to go through the eye of a needle than for someone who is rich to enter the kingdom of God" (Matt 19:23–24). The disciples are amazed because they have thought of wealth as being a sign of God's favor. Now they are learning that it could turn out to be an impediment in one's spiritual life.

## WHAT IS MY RESPONSIBILITY TOWARD OTHERS?

Still a third reason why accumulating wealth should not be a goal for a person who knows that "Jesus loves me" is that when one aspires to accumulate wealth, one often neglects acting as a steward over wealth and, therefore, neglects using it to serve those in need. This oversight is particularly likely to occur in a person who feels superior to those who are in need. Such blindness, such unwillingness to redistribute wealth, seems to be a fatal flaw in Jesus's eyes.

For example, when Jesus is teaching his disciples about the end times, when nations and people will be held accountable for their choices, he tells the parable of the judgment of the nations (Matt 25:31–46). In this parable, Jesus is teaching that those who feed the hungry, give drink to the thirsty, clothe the naked, care for the sick, and visit those in prison are invited into the kingdom. Those who fail to do so do not enter the kingdom. In failing to care for those in need, they have failed to serve their king.

By telling this parable, Jesus is teaching his disciples that God truly does love every individual. Those who realize this will joyfully realize that God loves them. But they will also realize that God loves the very people whom they are tempted not to love. They will realize that they are called to be witnesses of God's love to all of the marginalized. They are certainly not to use God or God's word to justify prejudicial actions toward other beloved children of God.

## AREN'T I GREAT!

As we have noted, it is not at all uncommon for sincerely religious people to feel superior to others. This is an age-old problem. Some of the disciples had the same problem. Luke tells us that the disciples started to argue about which one of them was the greatest. Jesus was aware of this and tried to teach them the total inappropriateness of the question. Jesus "took a little child and put it by his side, and said to them, 'Whoever welcomes this child in my name welcomes me, and whoever welcomes me welcomes the one who sent me; for the least among all of you is the greatest'" (Luke 9:48). The disciples are not to seek greatness in the world's understanding of greatness. Rather, they are simply to strive to be witnesses of Jesus's teachings in both word and deed and to serve those in need.

In addition, the disciples are not to get themselves puffed up with a sense of their own greatness in religious matters, as though they have earned the vocation and the spiritual gifts that they have received. Jesus teaches the disciples this through the parable of the vineyard workers (see Matt 20:1–16).

Jesus tells this parable in response to Peter who has said, "We have left everything and followed you. What then will we have" (Matt 19:27)? Jesus hears in Peter's question a false presumption, a sense that the disciples have earned eternal life rather than received it as an invitation and a gift. Jesus assures Peter that those who have followed Jesus will receive eternal life. Jesus says, "And everyone who has left houses or brothers or sisters or father or mother or children or fields for my name's sake, will receive a hundred-fold, and will inherit eternal life" (Matt 19:29). However, that does not mean that the disciples have earned this great gift.

The parable of the vineyard workers teaches Peter and the disciples that to receive eternal life is not to earn it by challenging their sense of earning. The problem presented through the parable is not that anyone fails to receive what that person has earned. The problem is that people get much more than they have earned.

In the parable, workers are hired to go into the vineyard to work at various times of the day. Those who are hired first are assured the usual daily wage. To be working in the vineyard is obviously a privilege: one has to be invited. This is made clear because toward the end of the day, the landowner sees some laborers who are not working. He asks them, "'Why are you standing here idle all day?' They say, 'Because no one has hired us'" (Matt

20:6b–20:7a). On hearing this, the landowner tells them that they also may go into the vineyard.

Trouble starts when the workers are paid. When the day is over, the workers leave in the order opposite to that of their hiring, and all the workers are paid the same daily wage. The all-day workers, who are aware that those who came later received the same wage as them, feel cheated, not because they were paid less than the daily wage they earned, but because the other workers were paid more than they earned.

Feeling fully justified in their anger, the all-day workers "grumble against the landowner" (Matt 20:11b). The landowner responds to one of them: "Friend, I am doing you no wrong; did you not agree with me for the usual daily wage? Take what belongs to you and go; I choose to give to this last the same as I give to you. Am I not allowed to do what I choose with what belongs to me? Or are you envious because I am generous" (Matt 20:13–15)?

As Peter hears this story, he will identify with the all-day workers, as do many of us when we hear the parable. The parable challenges the whole concept of earning. Peter revealed that he had mistakenly applied this concept to the spiritual life when he asked Jesus, "What then will I have?" Through the parable, Jesus is teaching Peter that he did not earn being called as a disciple any more than the workers earned being invited into the vineyard. The same is true for us. Whatever spiritual gifts we have received, we have received as gifts. We have not and cannot earn them. Therefore, as Jesus teaches Peter, spiritual gifts should be a source of gratitude, not of pride. Those who have received these gifts are not "greater" than others.

## DOES THE BIBLE TELL ME SO?

We see then, that while it is true that the Bible tells me that Jesus loves me, it is also true that Jesus loves everyone else. Therefore, to be in right relationship with God, I must be in right relationship with God's other beloved children: I must not judge or exclude others. I must always be willing to forgive others. I must share my material goods with those in need. I must not have wealth or worldly renown as goals. I must realize that I have not earned what I have; rather, I have received all things as gifts. Whenever I use Scripture to justify behavior that results in other people being marginalized or excluded, I am abusing Scripture. The measuring rod is love.

These conclusions are summed up in 1 John:

> Beloved, let us love one another, because love is from God; everyone who loves is born of God and knows God. Whoever does not love does not know God, for God is love. God's love was revealed among us in this way: God sent his only Son into the world so that we might live through him. In this is love, not that we loved God but that he loved us and sent his Son to be the atoning

sacrifice for our sins. Beloved, since God loved us so much, we also ought to love one another. No one has ever seen God; if we love one another, God lives in us, and his love is perfected in us. (1 John 4:7–12)

As we continue to ask, "Does the Bible tell me so?" in relation to a number of questions, we will find that those passages that appear to teach behavior that is unloving are the passages that are misunderstood because they are being read out of context. In order to understand what the passages are actually teaching, we will have to place them in the contexts of literary form, the beliefs of the time, and the process of revelation that is modeled for us in Scripture. Only then will we correctly understand the good news that has been revealed to us by Jesus Christ.

*Chapter Five*

# God Created the World in Six Days: The Theory of Evolution Is Incompatible with Scripture

*Does the Bible Tell Me So?*
*No*

Those who argue that the world was created in six days and that Darwin's theory of evolution is incompatible with Scripture fail to consider the contexts of literary form, the beliefs of the time of the author and audience, and the process of revelation. We broached this topic in Chapter 1 when discussing the contextualist approach to Scripture. We said then that the first story in the first book of the Bible, the story of creation in Genesis 1–2:4, is teaching us truths about our relationship with God, with each other, and with the rest of creation. It is not teaching us truths about science or history.

Because many people presume that the stories in the Bible are teaching the truth on every topic on the face of the earth, not just on the topics that the inspired authors are addressing, they use the Bible to answer questions that have nothing to do with the subject that the author is discussing. No biblical author is responding to the question: How old is the earth? To use Scripture to answer that question is to abuse Scripture.

To defend these claims, we will first put the story of creation as it appears in Genesis into context in order to understand what the inspired author was teaching his contemporary audience. That audience, as well as later generations, thought that this story taught universal, spiritual truths that every generation needed to hear. That is why it was passed on through the centuries and included in the canon. Only after we understand what the story is teaching will we discuss some of the ways the story is abused to address questions that have nothing to do with what the inspired author is teaching.

## WHAT IS GENESIS 1–2:4 TEACHING?

In the present arrangement of the stories in the Bible, the story of the creation of the world in six days appears first. However, these stories existed before the Bible took its present form and before the books were considered canonical (i.e., inspired by God and teaching revelatory truths about our relationship with God). Between the time of Abraham (1850 BC) and the time when the books in the Old Testament took their final form (after the Babylonian exile [587–537 BC] when the Israelites had returned to the holy land), the stories were edited and reedited several times in the light of subsequent experiences: after the exodus (1250 BC) and the settling in the holy land, after the split of the northern and southern kingdoms (922 BC), after the conquering of the northern kingdom by the Assyrians (721 BC), as well as after the Babylonian exile. While the story of creation comes first, it dates to the last editing period, after the Babylonian exile. The story was added as a preface to an already existing narrative.

Why is this important? To know the time in which a story was written is important because if we do not know the social setting of the author and audience we cannot understand the story in the context in which it was written. The story of creation in six days was written in response to some of the ideas to which the Israelites had been exposed while in Babylon.[1] For instance, the Babylonians believed in many gods, which included the sun and the moon. The Israelites believed in one God. The Babylonians believed that spirit was good but matter was not. The Israelites believed that God created the material world, and so it was good. The Babylonians believed that human beings were created from the corpse of a rebellious and defeated god. The Israelites believed in the goodness and dignity of each person. The Babylonians did not keep holy the Sabbath. For the Israelites, keeping holy the Sabbath was a very important part of living in fidelity to covenant love.

So, when the exiles returned to the holy land, they rebuilt their Temple, they edited their inherited stories, and they prefaced the connected narrative that we call the "book of Genesis" with the story of creation in six days, thus beginning the story by reaffirming their traditional beliefs.

The creation story is responding to the question: How did everything that exists get here? The author's answer is, "God created it." Because the theme of the story is that creation is God's work, the author selects a structure for the story that reinforces the theme: a workweek. In other words, the workweek is a literary device, a way of organizing the story. It is saying absolutely nothing about the amount of time that it took for the world as we know it to come into existence.

The author then pictures God creating all that exists in a very orderly way. For three days, God divides things: light from darkness, water above the firmament from water beneath the firmament, and water from dry land. On the next three days, God populates what has been divided: The sun, moon, and stars are put in the sky. Fish are put in the waters and birds in the sky. Animals and human beings are placed on the dry land. By the end of the sixth day, all has been created.

Obviously, the story is not teaching science. We now know what constitutes a day. It is the amount of time it takes the earth to rotate on its axis in relation to the sun. So, from a scientific point of view, we could not have a day before we have a sun. In this story, the sun and moon are not created until the fourth day. Does this mean that the story can't be true? Absolutely not. Why? —Because the word *truth* is not synonymous with scientific accuracy. A story in which God is the main character and human beings are not created until the sixth day is not presenting itself as history or science. We are dealing with an entirely different way of probing truth.

These observations bring us to the question of literary form. What kind of writing is the creation story? The story is probing a mystery: how everything that exists came into existence. A complete answer to that question is still beyond our comprehension. So the inspired author writes an imaginative and symbolic story in order to probe the mystery. In literary terms, this kind of writing is called *myth*.

In English-speaking countries, the use of the word *myth* often misleads people. The English language has two words spelled and pronounced as myth (a homonym). The most commonly used word *myth* is not the name of a literary form. It is a way of saying that something used to be believed but is now known to be false. If I say, "The idea that old people can't be healthy is just a myth," I am saying that it is untrue. This is not the word I am using to name the literary form of the creation story.

The literary form *myth* is defined as an imaginative and symbolic story about a reality that is beyond our comprehension. A myth orients us in a moral universe. As is true with any literary form, a myth can be a vehicle to teach truth as well as to teach falsehoods. For hundreds of generations, the communities that have received the myth that begins the book of Genesis have treasured it because of the profound truths that it teaches.

The inspired author presents us with one God. Contrary to the belief of the Babylonians, the sun and the moon are not gods. Rather, the sun and moon have been created by God to give light to the earth. To believe in one loving God is a great freedom over believing in many gods who are in competition with one another. In honoring one of many gods, a person might be angering the other gods. The Israelites had been called, since the time of Abraham, to live in fidelity to only one God.

Not only spirit, but also matter, is good. The inspired author emphasizes this truth over and over by having the words "And God saw that it was good" become a refrain in the story (see Gen 1:10, 12, 18, 25). To repeat something is to emphasize it: what God made is good. Again, to believe that the material world is God's creation, that it is good and that human beings are to receive it as a gift and with joy, is a great freedom. Many religious people through the centuries have needed to hear this good news.

In the Genesis creation story, human beings, both male and female are made in God's image: "So God created humankind in his image, / in the image of God he created them; / male and female he created them" (Gen 1:27). This God in whose image male and female are made is a loving God who wants human beings to flourish: "God blessed them, and God said to them, "Be fruitful and multiply, and fill the earth . . . " (Gen 1:28).

It is impossible to overemphasize the importance of this description. If both male and female are created in God's image, both are of equal dignity. If all people are created in God's image, then God loves every person and wants every person to flourish, not just a chosen few. This conviction that all human beings are made in God's image has come to be the root of all of our social-justice teachings. A person made in God's image should be treated with dignity, should not be someone's property, should not be exploited for a financial profit, should not live in poverty, and so forth. Once again, this teaching is very freeing. We are not essentially disordered people, made from the corpse of a rebellious, defeated god. We have the potential to become loving people because we have been made in the image of a loving God.

By using a workweek as his organizing structure, the author is able to once again teach the commandment originally given to Moses on Mt. Sinai: "Remember the Sabbath day and keep it holy. Six days you shall labor and do all your work. But the seventh day is a Sabbath to the Lord your God; you shall not do any work . . . " (Ex 20:8–9). To reinforce this teaching for the returned exiles, the author pictures God, too, resting on the Sabbath.

The lessons that the inspired author wanted to teach the returned exiles are just as true and just as essential for every generation as they were for the author's generation. There is one God. We must not worship false gods, be they the sun and the moon or money and power. God is the author of both the material and the spiritual worlds. We need not be suspicious of beauty or pleasure as though these gifts that we receive through the senses are distractions from God. Rather, they are gifts from God. We can believe that we have the potential to become loving people despite our flaws, which we know we have from experience. After all, we were created in the image of a loving God. We, too, would be wise to set aside one day a week to consciously honor God and grow in our relationship with God. As the Lord said to

Moses: "You shall keep my Sabbath, for this is a sign between me and you throughout your generations, given in order that you may know that I, the Lord, sanctify you" (Ex 31:12).

We see then that, while the creation story does not claim to teach history or science, it does claim to teach us eternal truths about our relationship with God. When we use the story to address questions that the author was not addressing, we not only abuse the Bible, but we also miss the truths that the inspired author was, and is, teaching.

## HOW IS THE CREATION STORY ABUSED?

The creation story is abused when it is used to respond to scientific or historical questions. Science studies material forms and recurring phenomena that can be observed and measured. Any story in which God is a character is not presenting itself as science because God is not a material form and God's presence and power in our lives cannot be measured. Historical accounts are about events that have been witnessed and about which we have either oral or written accounts. No person witnessed creation. Therefore, the story of creation remains silent in response to both scientific and historical questions.

Some creationists would reply to what I have just said by claiming that there was an eyewitness to creation: God was an eyewitness, and we have God's eyewitness account in the first story in Genesis.[2] This claim rests on a misunderstanding of the literary form of the story. The story is not in any way claiming that it is God's eyewitness account. God is not pictured as telling the story; God is a character in the story. In other words, the story is told in the third person by an inspired author who speaks as an omniscient narrator; it is not told in the first person by God.

This brings up the topic of just what Christians mean when we claim that in some sense God is the author of the Bible. To express this belief is not to claim that in the Bible we have God's eyewitness account of events, that God directly wrote the Bible, or even that God dictated the Bible for others to write. Rather, God revealed God's self through events. Inspired people witnessed those events and understood that they were events in which God was present and powerful. Inspired people thought and prayed about the significance of events and reached conclusions about God that they then taught others. Some people, like Abraham, Moses, Peter, and Paul had such profound experiences of God's presence that we would say they had visions.

However, Abraham did not write Genesis, Moses did not write Exodus, Peter did not write any of the Gospels, and Paul did not write Acts. As we explained earlier, when we read these works we are reading the fruit of oral, written, and edited traditions, the understanding of communities of faith through the centuries, not simply eyewitness accounts. To claim that God is the author of Scripture, then, is not to insist that Scripture contains God's eyewitness accounts. Nor is it to deny that the creation story in Genesis was written in the literary form *myth* by an inspired author who is teaching universal truths about our relationship with God.

So, while God is ultimately the author of Scripture, since God is Scripture's source, God worked through human beings. We cannot accurately claim that any book of the Bible is God's eyewitness account, unfiltered by human understanding.

## THE DISTINCTION BETWEEN
## SCIENCE AND THEOLOGY

The mistake that some are making today by using the Bible to argue against scientific theories is one that has a long history. The Catholic Church learned not to do this after condemning Galileo's teaching that the sun (heliocentricity), not the earth (geocentricity), is the center of planetary movement (1616).[3] Those who disagreed with Galileo used Scripture to argue against his theory.

In 1992, Pope John Paul II apologized for the Catholic Church's having condemned Galileo, acknowledging that Galileo had been right. The Pope said, "The majority of theologians did not recognize the formal distinction between Sacred Scripture and its interpretation, and this led them unduly to transpose into the realm of the doctrine of the faith a question which in fact pertained to scientific investigations."[4]

In our contemporary situation, the same mistake is being made. People are using the Bible to address scientific questions, thus abusing the Bible. Examining the passages used to argue against Galileo might explain more persuasively the absolute necessity of interpreting passages in context in order to understand the author's intent. Since we are no longer arguing over whether the sun or the earth is the center of planetary movement, we can more readily see that those who used Scripture to argue against Galileo, and to claim that the earth was not moving, were changing the subject entirely. The original authors were not addressing the question that they were using the passages to address.

Among the passages used to argue against Galileo's theory that the earth was moving around the sun are the following:

"The Lord is king, he is robed in majesty; the Lord is robed, he is girded with strength, / He established the world; it shall never be moved" (Ps 93:1).

"Say among the nations, 'The Lord is king! / The world is firmly established; it shall never be moved" (Ps 96:10).

"You set the earth on its foundations, / so that it shall never be shaken" (Ps 104:5).

"The sun rises and the sun goes down, / and hurries to the place where it rises" (Eccles 1:5).

In the passages from the Psalms, the inspired authors are extolling God's greatness, God's rule, God's reliability. The authors are teaching that God is king. In the course of doing this, they use as evidence the permanence of God's creation. The authors do presume that the earth is not in motion, but they are not teaching that the earth is not in motion.

In the passage from Ecclesiastes, the author is talking about the vanity of all things: "Vanity of vanities, says the Teacher, vanity of vanities! All is vanity" (Eccles 1:2)! To illustrate his point, he names many things in creation that just keep repeating themselves: generations come and go, the sun rises and sets and rises again, the wind keeps blowing, and streams run to the sea.

Even though we now know that the earth is rotating on its axis in relation to the sun, we still speak of the sun as rising and setting because that is the way it appears from our point of view. When we say that, we are not trying to address a scientific question. Neither were the inspired biblical authors. None of them was addressing the question that their words were later used to address.

Does the Bible teach us that God created the world in six days? No. The Bible does not address this scientific question. Does the Bible contradict Darwin's theory of evolution? No. Whether Darwin's theory is right or wrong, the Bible remains silent on this question. The creation story is teaching truth, but it is not teaching scientific truth. Rather, it is teaching us about the creative and loving nature of our one God who is the source of all that exists and about our own dignity as people who have been made in God's own image.

## NOTES

1. For a fuller discussion of this topic see Margaret Nutting Ralph, *And God Said What? An Introduction to Biblical Literary Forms* (Mahwah, NJ: Paulist Press, 2003) 29–38.

2. This view was defended by Ken Ham, a creationist, in his February 5, 2014, debate with Bill Nye, a scientist. See www.youtube.com/watch?v=z6kgvhG3Akl (accessed May 11, 2014).

3. For more details on this controversy, written from the point of view of a defense of the Catholic Church, see "The Galileo Controversy" at http://www.catholic.com/tractrs/the-galileo-controversy (accessed May 12, 2014).

4. John Paul II, "Faith Can Never Conflict with Reason," speech to the Pontifical Academy of Sciences (October 31, 1992), reported *in L'Osservatore Romano* (November 4, 1992), para. 9, http://www.unigre.it/cssf/comuni/documenti/chiesa/Galilei.html (site discontinued).

## Chapter Six

# Homosexual People Cannot Marry

*Does the Bible Tell Me So?*
*No*

It is so much easier to demonstrate the ways in which the Bible is abused when discussing a question that is no longer debated. None of us would use the Bible today to argue that slavery is moral, that women should not vote, or that the earth is the center of the Solar System and remains stable. Some people do still use the Bible to support their belief that the earth is only six thousand years old or that evolution is a false theory. However, this is not an issue where our differences in understanding deprive those on either side of the argument of their civil rights. Much more contentious is the present disagreement about the Supreme Court's decision that homosexual people should be allowed to legally marry in the United States. Is sexual activity between married homosexuals an abomination? Is it sinful? Is even discussing this topic evidence of how secularized life in the United States has become?

Many people believe that the Bible clearly forbids and condemns homosexual activity. In this chapter, we will look at the biblical passages that are used to argue against homosexual marriage and determine whether the original inspired authors are responding to the question that we are now asking. To do this, we will use the same method of inquiry that we have used in previous chapters: we will examine context in order to determine meaning.

# THE QUESTION TO BE ADDRESSED

Before we turn to Scripture to see if it is responding to today's question, let us first define the question. The question we are addressing is: Is marriage between committed homosexual people moral or immoral? This is a different question, but related to: Should marriage between committed homosexual people be legal or illegal? The second question relates to civil society and to civil rights. However, those who oppose making marriage between homosexuals legal often oppose it on moral grounds. They believe that the Bible forbids such relationships, and they see the acceptance of marriage between people of the same sex as a sign of the moral disintegration of society.

To discuss this question, we must take into consideration the fact that the word *homosexuality* as well as the concept behind it was not part of the English language until the last decade of the nineteenth century. While science has not yet determined why some people's sexual orientation is toward members of their own sex rather than to the opposite sex, science has determined that human sexuality appears as a continuum: some people find that their sexual attraction is to the opposite sex, some find that it is to both sexes, and some find that it is to the same sex. The orientation itself is not chosen.

When the fact that some people are homosexual was realized and named, homosexuality was often regarded as a disorder. In fact, until 1973, homosexuality was listed as a mental disorder in the American Psychiatric Association's *Diagnostic and Statistical Manual of Mental Disorders* (*DSM*). However, psychiatrists and psychologists (since 1975) now agree that homosexuality is a normal expression of human sexuality. Both of their associations agree that to discriminate against people because of their sexual orientation is to do them harm.

The fact that the concept of a homosexual orientation and the word naming it have been part of human knowledge and discourse for only a little over one hundred years means that the question "Is marriage between committed homosexual people moral or immoral?" is never addressed in Scripture. The inspired authors knew nothing about homosexual orientation. Just as many committed Christians do not accept the scientific evidence that the earth is much older than previously thought (see Chapter 5), many do not accept as fact the knowledge that science offers us about homosexuality. When reading the Bible, they presume that the authors are addressing their questions about homosexuality, when in fact the authors are addressing other questions pertinent to their contemporary audiences.

As discussed in Chapter 4, Christians do not want to discriminate against others because Jesus, who Christians believe is God's own self-revelation and is our model, has taught us to go out of our way to love and embrace the very people whom society wants to marginalize. However, since Christians believe that the Bible is inspired, they must come to terms with the passages that some cite as forbidding marriage between homosexual people. What were the inspired authors teaching in these passages?

## OLD TESTAMENT PASSAGES USED TO ARGUE AGAINST HOMOSEXUAL MARRIAGE

The first passage in the Old Testament that those who argue against homosexual marriage cite is from Genesis 1:27: "So God created humankind in his image, / in the image of God he created them; / male and female he created them." Jesus is pictured as quoting this passage in the Gospels. For instance, in Mark 10:6–9, Jesus says, "But from the beginning of creation, 'God made them male and female.' 'For this reason a man shall leave his father and mother and be joined to his wife, and the two shall become one flesh.' So they are no longer two, but one flesh. Therefore what God has joined together, let no one separate" (see also Matt 19:4–6).

In Chapter 5 we discussed at length what the creation story in Genesis is teaching. This passage has immense importance because it pictures God making both the male and female in God's own image, not just males. The lesson from this passage is that all human beings are made in God's image and are therefore people of great dignity and importance. The passage is not addressing our question regarding homosexual marriage, and the concept of sexual orientation was completely unknown to the inspired author.

Mark tells us specifically what question Jesus was answering when he spoke of marriage being between a man and a woman. The Pharisees did not ask Jesus anything about homosexual people, a concept completely unknown to them. Rather, their question was on the topic of divorce. They ask, "Is it lawful for a man to divorce his wife" (Mark 10:2)? Jesus asks the Pharisees, who are experts in the law, what Moses had commanded. The Pharisees respond that Moses "allows a man to write a certificate of dismissal and to divorce her" (Mark 10:4). Jesus tells the Pharisees that in this instance, the law is not demanding enough. A man should not dismiss his wife: ". . . what God has joined together, let no one separate" (Mark 10:9). Here Jesus was defending the rights of women who, if dismissed, would be marginalized in society. Even though men had authority over women and could dismiss them, they should not do so, especially for the kind of trivial reasons that were allowed at that time.

We see then that neither the passage from Genesis nor Jesus's quoting the passage from Genesis in response to the Pharisees' question can be used to answer our question about the morality of homosexual marriage. However, Jesus's response to the Pharisees is pertinent for another modern-day question: Is divorce moral or immoral? We will address this question in a later chapter.

A second passage from the book of Genesis that is often quoted to condemn homosexual marriage is the story of Sodom and Gomorrah (Gen 19:1–11). In this story, the men of Sodom want to gang rape Lot's guests. The men call to Lot, "Where are the men who came to you tonight? Bring them out to us, so that we may know them" (Gen 19:5). Lot will not allow the men to gang rape his guests, but he does offer his daughters instead. Lot says, "I beg you, my brothers, do not act so wickedly. Look, I have two daughters who have not known a man; let me bring them out to you, and do to them as you please; only do nothing to these men . . . " (Gen 19:7–8).

This story is illustrating the sinfulness of Sodom, which will be destroyed. As the story continues, it will also illustrate God's faithfulness to his promises to Abraham. While the wicked city is destroyed, Lot, who is Abraham's nephew, is saved (Gen 19:29). Obviously, the story says nothing at all about marriage between homosexuals. The sexual behavior condemned here is gang rape of male guests, not homosexual sex in the context of marriage.

The final Old Testament passages that are used to argue against homosexual marriage appear in the holiness code in Leviticus (Lev 17–26). The specific passages in question are "You shall not lie with a male as with a woman; it is an abomination" (Lev 18:22) and "If a man lies with a male as with a woman, both of them have committed an abomination; they shall be put to death; their blood is upon them" (Lev 20:13).

The holiness code instructs the Israelites on how to be holy as God is holy, on how to be separate from and different from their non-Israelite neighbors. God tells Moses: "Speak to the people of Israel and say to them: I am the Lord your God. You shall not do as they do in the land of Egypt, where you lived, and you shall not do as they do in the land of Canaan, to which I am bringing you. You shall not follow their statutes" (Lev 18:2–3).

The passages we are discussing are in the context of instructions on how to obey God's statutes regarding the sanctuary and sacrifice. We can tell that this is the context of the instruction that a male should not lie down with a male because the sentence before that one is: "You shall not give any of your offspring to sacrifice them to Molech, and so profane the name of your God" (Lev 18:21). In other words, the Israelites were not to practice child sacrifice.

The Israelites were also not to engage in the kind of fertility rites practiced by the Egyptians and the Canaanites. These involved the use of both male and female prostitutes. The pagans believed that such actions in honor of the gods increased the fertility of the land. Deuteronomy specifically forbids such behavior: "None of the daughters of Israel shall be a temple prostitute; none of the sons of Israel shall be a temple prostitute" (Deut 23:17). Nevertheless, the practice of having cult prostitutes continued. As we read in 1 Kings, King Jeroboam "put away the male temple prostitutes out of the land, and removed all the idols that his ancestors had made" (1 Kings 15:12). The same kind of reform was necessary under King Jehoshaphat:

"The remnant of the male temple prostitutes who were still in the land in the days of his father Asa, he exterminated" (1 Kings 22:46).

We see then that the instruction that a male not lie down with a male is forbidding men to use male prostitutes in fertility rites. It says nothing at all in response to the question we are asking about homosexual marriage.

## NEW TESTAMENT PASSAGES USED TO ARGUE AGAINST HOMOSEXUAL MARRIAGE

The Gospels say nothing more on our topic than we have already discussed. However, three of the letters do: 1 Corinthians, Romans, and 1 Timothy. These are the passages that need to be discussed.

Paul, in his letter to the Corinthians says: "Do you not know that wrong-doers will not inherit the kingdom of God? Do not be deceived! Fornicators, idolaters, adulterers, male prostitutes, sodomites, thieves, the greedy, drunkards, revilers, robbers—none of these will inherit the kingdom of God" (1 Cor 6:9–10).

In Romans Paul says, "For this reason God gave them up to degrading passions. Their women exchanged natural intercourse for unnatural, and in the same way also the men, giving up natural intercourse with women, were consumed with passion for one another. Men committed shameless acts with men and received in their own persons the due penalty for their error" (Rom 1:26–27).

In 1 Timothy we read: "This means understanding that the law is laid down not for the innocent but for the lawless and disobedient, for the godless and sinful, for the unholy and profane, for those who kill their father or mother, for murderers, fornicators, sodomites, slave traders, liars, perjurers, and whatever else is contrary to the sound teaching that conforms to the glorious gospel of the blessed God, which he entrusted to me" (1 Tim 1:9–11).

We will discuss 1 Corinthians and 1 Timothy together because each letter uses the same Greek word that is translated here as *sodomites*. The New American Bible translates the word in question as *practicing homosexuals*. Since neither the word *homosexual* nor the concept behind it was part of anyone's understanding until about one hundred years ago, that translation is misleading. The Greek word in question is αρσενοκοιται (arseno [male] koitai [bed]). Scripture scholars surmise that the word is referring to adult males who use boy prostitutes. In 1 Corinthians, *male prostitutes* appears right before *sodomites*. If this is the meaning, the condemned behavior is what our culture calls "child abuse": an adult male having sex with a child.

Paul's letter to the Romans, however, does not appear to be about fertility rites or sexual relationships with boy prostitutes. In Romans 1:26–27, Paul is listing sins that the Gentiles have committed. Paul says, "So they are without excuse; for though they knew God, they did not honor him as God or give thanks to him, but they became futile in their thinking, and their senseless minds were darkened" (Rom 1:20–21). The result was that the Gentiles sinned. In addition to sexual sins, they "were filled with every kind of wickedness, evil, covetousness, malice. Full of envy, murder, strife, deceit, craftiness, they are gossips, slanderers, God-haters, insolent, haughty, boastful, inventors of evil, rebellious toward parents, foolish faithless, heartless, ruthless" (Rom 1:29–32).

What are the sexual sins to which Paul refers? Here the sin does seem to be sexual relationships between adults of the same sex: men "give up" natural intercourse with women and, consumed with passion, commit shameless acts with each other. Remember, however, that Paul has never heard of a homosexual orientation. He pictures heterosexuals "giving up natural intercourse" to do something that Paul understands to be completely unnatural. In addition, Paul is describing behavior that is based on lust, not love. These sinners are "consumed with passion for one another." Paul is talking about promiscuity, not expressions of love within a committed relationship.

It is, therefore, accurate to say that no biblical passage responds to the specific question that we are asking because no biblical author had any idea that some people's sexual orientation was toward members of their own sex. The Bible remains silent when it comes to specifically forbidding or approving of marriage between homosexual people.

Those who accept the authority of Scripture but also accept the goodness of homosexual marriage apply core concepts of Scripture to a new social setting. Believing that all human beings need to love and be loved, and believing that a homosexual orientation is part of the natural order (knowledge that was not available to inspired biblical authors), they conclude that a committed, faithful relationship of lifelong love is just as valid for a homosexual person as it is for a heterosexual person. The state should not deprive homosexual individuals of the rights that heterosexual individuals receive, including the right to marry. To do so would be to unjustly discriminate against them.

Does the Bible tell me that marriage between homosexual people is sinful? The Bible does not. The Bible names gang rape, sexual relations as part of fertility rites, sexual relations with prostitutes, and unnatural sexual relations based in lust as sins. The Bible remains silent on the morality of marriage between people whose sexual orientation is homosexual.

## Chapter Seven

# Divorce and Remarriage Is Always Wrong: There Are No Exceptions

*Does the Bible Tell Me So?*
*No*

In our last chapter, we quoted Jesus's response to the Pharisees who asked him whether it was acceptable for a man to divorce his wife. After acknowledging that the Law does allow a man to divorce his wife, Jesus attributes this teaching to people's hardness of heart. Jesus then says: "But from the beginning of creation, God made them male and female. For this reason a man shall leave his father and mother and be joined to his wife, and the two shall become one flesh. So they are no longer two, but one flesh. Therefore what God has joined together, let no one separate" (Mark 10:6–9). Later, in conversation with the disciples, Jesus adds to this teaching, saying: "Whoever divorces his wife and marries another commits adultery against her; and if she divorces her husband and marries another, she commits adultery" (Mark 10:11).

This passage, taken by itself, seems to be an iron-clad teaching: to divorce one's spouse and marry another is always wrong. However, this is not the only place in the New Testament where the question of divorce is addressed. In some other passages, exceptions are made.

## AN EXCEPTION IN MATTHEW

Scripture scholars believe that Matthew used Mark as a source. This is very valuable information because it means that if Matthew tells a story that also appears in Mark, but the accounts are not the same, Matthew has purposeful-ly altered his source for pastoral reasons. Matthew does repeat Mark's inter-change between the Pharisees and Jesus on the question of divorce. However, in Matthew, the question is slightly different, and Jesus's answer is slightly different.

Instead of asking Jesus, "Is it lawful for a man to divorce his wife" (Mark 10:2), the Pharisees ask, "Is it lawful for a man to divorce his wife for any cause?" (Matt 19:3). The Jewish Law did allow a man to divorce his wife, sometimes for trivial reasons. Jesus, of course, knows this and once more attributes such permission to people's hardheartedness. Jesus then goes on to say, "And I say to you, whoever divorces his wife, except for unchastity, and marries another, commits adultery" (Matt 19:9).

Obviously, Matthew has introduced an exception to the blanket prohibi-tion against divorce. However, Scripture scholars debate exactly what the exception is. While the New Revised Standard Version (NRSV) uses the word *unchastity* to translate *porneia*, the word found in the Greek manu-scripts (the root word for the English word *pornography*), other translations use words such as *fornication* (the Jerusalem Bible), *unlawful* marriage (the New American Bible), and *unfaithfulness* (the Good News Bible). The words used to translate *porneia* are obviously not synonyms. This leaves us with the question: What, exactly, is Matthew's exception?

Whatever the exception, Matthew has earlier pictured Jesus making it in his Sermon on the Mount. When teaching on divorce Jesus says: "It was also said, 'Whoever divorces his wife, let him give her a certificate of divorce.' But I say to you that anyone who divorces his wife, except on the grounds of unchastity, causes her to commit adultery; and whoever marries a divorced woman commits adultery" (Matt 5:31–32).

In trying to solve this problem, Scripture scholars look to other parts of the New Testament for clues. Between the time of Jesus's preaching and Matthew's Gospel (80 AD), the question regarding divorce was asked not just in the context of the Jewish world and the Jewish Law (the social context for any conversation between Jesus and the Pharisees) but also in the context of the Gentile world. The Jews had laws of consanguinity: people of a certain degree of kinship, such as a brother and sister, could not marry (see Lev 18:6–18). The Gentiles did not have these laws. What, then, should one do if a Gentile who was married contrary to the Jewish laws of consanguinity wanted to become a Christian? Should that marriage be allowed to continue?

Scripture scholars suggest that the dissolution of a Gentile marriage that violates Jewish consanguinity laws is Matthew's exception. Evidence that such laws were applied to Gentiles appears in Acts. At the Council of Jerusa-lem, the early Church met to decide what parts of the Jewish law would be binding on Gentiles who became Christians. Would they have to be circum-cised? According to Acts, circumcision was not required, but some dietary laws and some consanguinity laws were required. James announces these decisions: "For it has seemed good to the Holy Spirit and to us to impose on you no further burden than these essentials: that you abstain from what has been sacrificed to idols and from blood and from what is strangled and from fornication. If you keep yourselves from these, you will do well. Farewell" (Acts 15:28–29). Scripture scholars surmise that the word translated as *fornication* in this passage refers to Gentile marriages that violate the Jewish consanguinity laws. The New American Bible's translation reflects this understanding. In this translation, it is not "fornication" that is forbidden, but "unlawful marriage" (Acts 15:29).

## THE SECOND EXCEPTION

A second exception to the teaching against divorce and remarriage appears in Paul's first letter to the Corinthians. Paul acknowledges Jesus's teaching on the matter but, in a different social setting, also feels free to make an exception. First Paul says: "To the married I give this command—not I but the Lord—that the wife should not separate from her husband (but if she does separate, let her remain unmarried or else be reconciled to her husband), and that the husband should not divorce his wife" (1 Cor 7:10–11).

However, Paul does not stop there. He continues:

> To the rest I say—I and not the Lord—that if any believer has a wife who is an unbeliever, and she consents to live with him, he should not divorce her. And if any woman has a husband who is an unbeliever, and he consents to live with her, she should not divorce him. For the unbelieving husband is made holy through his wife, and the unbelieving wife is made holy through her husband. Otherwise your children would be unclean, but as it is, they are holy. But if the unbelieving partner separates, let it be so; in such a case the brother or sister is not bound. It is to peace that God has called you. (1 Cor 7:12–15)

So Paul is affirming Jesus's teaching. However, he does make an exception. If an unbelieving spouse leaves a believing spouse (not the believing spouse's choice), then the believing spouse is free. In the Catholic Church's annulment process, this exception is still recognized and is called the Pauline Privilege.

## THE IDEAL OF MARRIAGE

Why is the question of divorce such a serious one in Christian contexts? Why did Jesus emphasize that the Jewish law did not regard marriage seriously enough, allowing men to dismiss their wives for trivial reasons? As we have seen, in supporting his teaching, Jesus quotes Genesis, claiming that the union of husband and wife was established by God, and that what God has joined together, human beings should not separate (Mark 10:9). The same concept, the permanence of marriage, is also taught in the letter to the Ephesians, in which the relationship between husband and wife is held up as a model of the relationship between Christ and the Church. We quoted some of this passage in an earlier chapter because parts of it were abused to argue against women's suffrage.

Ephesians says:

> Be subject to one another out of reverence for Christ. Wives, be subject to your husbands as you are to the Lord. For the husband is the head of the wife just as Christ is the head of the church, the body of which he is the Savior. Just as the church is subject to Christ, so wives ought to be, in everything, to their husbands.
>
> Husbands, love your wives, just as Christ loved the church and gave himself up for her, in order to make her holy by cleansing her with the washing of water by the word, so as to present the church to himself in splendor, without a spot or wrinkle or anything of the kind—yes, so that she may be holy and without blemish. In the same way, husbands should love their wives as they do their own bodies. He who loves his wife loves himself. For no one ever hates his own body, but he nourishes and tenderly cares for it, just as Christ does for the church, because we are members of his body. "For this reason, a man will leave his father and mother and be joined to his wife, and the two will become one flesh." This is a great mystery, and I am applying it to Christ and the church (Eph 5:21–34).

As we explained in Chapter 3, the author of Ephesians is writing a letter to people who lived in a social order in which wives and slaves were property. Given that setting, he is teaching husbands, wives, children, slaves, and masters how to love one another as Christ has loved them.

In the process of applying Jesus's teaching that we must love one another to this particular social setting, the author draws an analogy between the relationship of a husband and wife and the relationship of Christ and the Church. Marriage is to be a living symbol, a witness to the community, of Christ's covenant love for the Church. Just as the relationship between Christ and the Church can never be broken, the relationship between husband and wife can never be broken because husband and wife have become one, just as Christ and the Church are one: Husband and wife are one body; the Church is the body of Christ.

The ideal of marriage presented in this passage remains in the Church today. Both the Catholic Church and the Orthodox Church consider marriage a *sacrament*. The New Testament does not use the word *sacrament*, which Augustine defined as a visible sign of an invisible reality. Rather, as we see here, Ephesians uses the word *mystery*. To this day, *mystery* remains the word for *sacrament* in the Eastern Orthodox Church. Sacraments are called

*Holy Mysteries.* The two words function as synonyms because, in the early third century, Tertullian translated the Greek word *musterion* into Latin as *sacramentum.*

What does the author of Ephesians mean to teach when he uses the word *mystery* in relation to the union of a husband and wife? The author explains what he means earlier in the letter. By *mystery*, the author means God's plan of salvation, which was once hidden but has now been revealed through Jesus Christ. Ephesians says: "With all wisdom and insight [God] has made known to us the mystery of his will, according to his good pleasure that he set forth in Christ, as a plan for the fullness of time, to gather up all things to him, things in heaven and things on earth" (Eph 1:8b–10; see also 3:3 and 3:9).

When the author of Ephesians says, "This is a great mystery, and I am applying it to Christ and the Church," he is saying that marriage reveals in a tangible way God's will for God's people: it is God's will that we live in love. One way the mystery of God's love is revealed to spouses, to children, indeed to all of society, is through the mystery, the sacrament, of marriage.

However, this high ideal of mystery that reveals God's love is not always the reality experienced by people who are legally married. That is why Paul makes an exception to Jesus's teaching on marriage in the case of a person who has been deserted by his or her spouse. That is why the Catholic Church does not consider a legal marriage synonymous with a sacramental marriage. It is simply a sad reality of life that not all legal marriages are mysteries that reveal God's love to God's people. In a civil context, this sad truth is acknowledged through divorce, a dissolution of a legally binding contract. In the Catholic Church setting, it is acknowledged through annulment, a recognition that a sacramental marriage did not exist.

We see, then, that the Bible presents us with the highest possible ideal of what marriage should be: a living witness of God's love for God's people and for Christ's love for the Church. However, the Bible also acknowledges experience: Jesus, in Matthew's Gospel, and Paul in 1 Corinthians introduce exceptions to the ideal. So, while the Bible teaches the holiness of marriage, it does not teach that divorce and remarriage are always wrong. There are some exceptions.

*Chapter Eight*

# Christ Is Present in Eucharist

*Does the Bible Tell Me So?*
*Yes*

Central to Christian worship is the celebration of Eucharist. While all Christians celebrate Eucharist, not all Christians agree on just what is happening when we celebrate it. Through the centuries, theologians have discussed such questions as: Is Christ truly present in Eucharist, or is the ritual a remembrance of Christ's past presence and a hope in Christ's future coming? If Christ is present, just how is he present? Do the elements of bread and wine change into Christ's body and blood, or is Christ's presence in the community that has gathered in Christ's name, rather than in the elements themselves? What is the effect of celebrating Eucharist?

In this chapter, we will not turn to theologians, such as Augustine or Thomas Aquinas, to probe the mystery of Eucharist. We will not use Greek philosophical categories of thought, such as *transubstantiation*, to teach doctrine. Rather, we will look at the many ways in which inspired biblical authors probe this mystery, using a wide variety of narrative forms. [1] We will find that Scripture does teach that by receiving Eucharist, we participate in an intimate relationship with the risen Christ, a relationship that accomplishes profound unity and is accompanied by serious responsibilities. The Bible does tell us so.

## EUCHARIST IN PAUL

The earliest account we have of the significance of Eucharist appears in Paul's first letter to the Corinthians. Paul wrote 1 Corinthians about 56 AD, so this letter predates the other accounts of Eucharist that we have in the New Testament. (Mark, the earliest of our Gospels, dates to about 65 AD) As stated in Chapter 3, when Paul wrote the Corinthians, he was writing people whom he knew well. Paul had established the Church in Corinth during his second missionary journey (Acts 18:1–28) and had obviously taught the Corinthians to celebrate Eucharist. We can tell this because, instead of teaching Christ's presence in Eucharist, Paul presumes that they already know this.

In 1 Corinthians 7:1–14:40, Paul is addressing some questions that have arisen since he left Corinth, questions about issues that are presently causing division in the community. One of these questions is whether it is acceptable to eat the meat of an animal sacrificed to idols before being sold in the market. As part of his argument, Paul wants to remind the Corinthians of the unity that they have in Christ. Paul says: "The cup of blessing that we bless, is it not a sharing in the blood of Christ? The bread that we break, is it not a sharing in the body of Christ? Because there is one bread, we who are many are one body, for we all partake of the one bread" (1 Cor 10:15–17).

Here Paul is reminding the Corinthians of something they already know: when they receive Eucharist, they are receiving the *body and blood* of Christ, Paul's way of saying the *person* of Christ. Christ is actually present. Paul is reminding the Corinthians of this core truth in order to build on this knowledge. Paul wants to teach the ramifications of having been united with Christ in Eucharist. Those ramifications include the fact that Christians who receive the body of Christ share a profound unity in Christ that gives them responsibility for each other. Therefore, the Corinthians must consider not only their freedom of action but also how their actions affect others, not only their freedom to eat the questionable meat but also whether eating the meat will give offense to others.

Paul then moves on to discuss problems that have arisen in the way the Corinthians are celebrating Eucharist. Evidently, when the Corinthians were gathering for Eucharist in their homes, they were not taking responsibility for the poor in their midst. Paul says: "For when the time comes to eat, each of you goes ahead with your own supper, and one goes hungry and another becomes drunk. What? Do you not have homes to eat and drink in? Or do you show contempt for the church of God and humiliate those who have nothing?" (1 Cor 10:21–22a).

It is during this discussion that Paul gives us our earliest description of the institution of Eucharist:

> "For I received from the Lord what I also handed on to you, that the Lord Jesus on the night when he was betrayed took a loaf of bread, and when he had given thanks, he broke it and said, 'This is my body that is for you. Do this in remembrance of me.' In the same way he took the cup also, after supper,

saying, 'This cup is the new covenant in my blood. Do this, as often as you drink it, in remembrance of me.' For as often as you eat this bread and drink the cup, you proclaim the Lord's death until he comes." (1 Cor 11:23–26)

Here Paul makes clear that when Christians celebrate Eucharist, in addition to becoming one with Christ and with each other, they are proclaiming the salvific effect of Christ's death, the "new covenant in [Christ's] blood." They are also proclaiming the eschatological nature of the meal in that they "proclaim the Lord's death until he comes." All of God's covenant promises to God's people are being fulfilled through the risen Christ.

The unity in Christ that is accomplished through Eucharist gives those who receive Christ a profound responsibility for each other. Paul is very upset with the Corinthians because they do not seem to understand this. Paul says, "Whoever, therefore, eats the bread or drinks the cup of the Lord in an unworthy manner will be answerable for the body and blood of the Lord. Examine yourselves, then eat of the bread and drink of the cup. For all who eat and drink without discerning the body eat and drink judgment against themselves" (1 Cor 11:27–29).

The "body" that the Corinthians are failing to discern is not the presence of Christ in Eucharist (as we have seen, that is a given), but the one body that those who have received Eucharist have become: the body of Christ that is the Church. By ignoring the poor in their midst, the Corinthians are failing to recognize the body of Christ in the poor and therefore are receiving Eucharist unworthily. They are responsible for the body and blood of Christ. So are we.

Later in 1 Corinthians, Paul elaborates on the fact that those who are baptized into Christ and who receive the body of Christ become the body of Christ. When discussing the idea that all of the Corinthians have spiritual gifts that they have been given in order to serve the community, Paul says: "For just as the body is one and has many members, and all the members of the body, though many, are one body, so it is with Christ. For in the one Spirit we were all baptized into one body—Jews or Greeks, slaves or free— and we were all made to drink of one Spirit. . . . Now you are the body of Christ and individually members of it" (1 Cor 12:12–13, 27).

It is because the Corinthians are one body in Christ that Paul is so upset with them for not recognizing their unity when they celebrate Eucharist, of all things. They are privileged to receive the body of Christ. They must learn to recognize that they have become the body of Christ and are to continue Christ's proclamation of the good news in action as well as in words, especially when they gather for Eucharist.

## EUCHARIST IN LUKE

Christ's presence in Eucharist is core to Luke's Gospel. Not only does Luke include an account of Jesus instituting Eucharist at his last meal with the disciples, the Passover meal,[2] but he also teaches (through his infancy narrative) that Jesus is truly food for the flock and (through his story of the two disciples on the road to Emmaus) that Jesus remains with his people, especially in Eucharist. Christ's presence in Eucharist is an ever-present theme in Luke's Gospel.

## LUKE'S INFANCY NARRATIVE

An infancy narrative is a distinct literary form. It does not respond to the request: "Tell me exactly what happened." Rather, it responds to the request: "Tell me just how great this person became as you know from hindsight." Infancy narratives developed late in the Gospel tradition. Only Matthew and Luke include infancy narratives in their Gospels. Only Luke pictures Jesus being born in a manger. Luke has two purposes in doing this. One is to teach the significance of Jesus's birth by using a literary device known as *midrash*; the other is to teach something about Eucharist.

Both Matthew and Luke employ midrash in their birth narratives. That is, they weave into their accounts of Jesus's birth plot elements that are allusions to Old Testament texts. Their purpose in doing this is to teach the significance of Jesus's birth as it was understood after the resurrection. It is because Matthew and Luke both employ midrash that their infancy narratives differ so much in details. For example, only Matthew has the star and the wise men. Only Luke has the manger and the announcement to the shepherds. In explaining the significance of Jesus Christ's birth as it was understood after the resurrection, they allude to different Old Testament texts.

When Luke places Jesus's birth in a manger, he is alluding to the beginning of the book of Isaiah. Isaiah presents God as bemoaning the fact that the people do not know God. God says:

> The ox knows its owner,
> and the donkey its master's crib;
> but Israel does not know,
> my people do not understand. (Is 1:3)

By placing Jesus in a manger, having the angel announce Jesus's birth to the shepherds, and having the shepherds recognize their savior (Luke 2:1–20), Luke is teaching that the situation described in Isaiah has been reversed through Jesus Christ. God's people now do recognize their God.

In addition, by placing Jesus in a manger, Luke is teaching something about Eucharist. In Luke's account, the shepherds are told, ". . . to you is born this day in the city of David a Savior, who is the Messiah, the Lord. This will be a sign for you: you will find a child wrapped in bands of cloth and lying in a manger" (Luke 2:11–12). When the shepherds follow the angel's instructions, they find "Mary and Joseph, and the child lying in the manger" (Luke 2:16). By having the angel tell the shepherds that the infant lying in the manger is a *sign*, Luke is teaching us to look for a deeper meaning. What does this sign signify?

A manger is the place where one puts food for the flock. By placing Jesus in the manger, Luke is teaching that Jesus is food for the flock. Jesus nourishes us, gives us strength, and accompanies us on all of life's journeys. We are never alone. We are never without the presence of our Lord, Messiah, and Savior whom we receive in Eucharist. This theme will be emphasized again in Luke in the story of the two disciples on the road to Emmaus.

## LUKE'S PASSOVER MEAL

Luke's account of Jesus's last meal with his disciples has a great deal in common with the account that we read in Paul. However, Luke, like Mark and Matthew, pictures Jesus instituting Eucharist at the Passover meal, thus reinterpreting the meaning of the celebration. The Passover meal, of course, was a celebration of the Exodus, of God's protecting the Israelites so that the angel of death *passed over* their firstborns, thus allowing the people to *pass over* from slavery to freedom. The Eucharistic meal that Jesus initiates will celebrate his passing through death to new life, thus making it possible for his disciples to *pass over* from slavery to sin and death, and to enter eternal life.

Like Paul, Luke emphasizes the eschatological nature of Eucharist. Jesus says, "'I have eagerly desired to eat this Passover with you before I suffer; for I tell you, I will not eat it until it is fulfilled in the kingdom of God.' Then he took a cup, and after giving thanks he said, 'Take this and divide it among yourselves for I tell you that from now on I will not drink of the fruit of the vine until the kingdom of God comes'" (Luke 22:15–18). As we will soon see, this story foreshadows the post-resurrection appearance story when the disciples recognize that it is the risen Christ who has joined them for a meal (Luke 24:31). Once more, heaven and earth are joined.

Also like Paul, Luke emphasizes the proclamation of the salvific effect of Jesus's passion, death, and resurrection. Luke tells us that Jesus "took a loaf of bread, and when he had given thanks, he broke it and gave it to them, saying, 'This is my body, which is given for you. Do this in remembrance of me'" (Luke 22:19). This scene, too, foreshadows the risen Christ's actions with the two disciples whom he joins on the road to Emmaus: the risen Christ will take bread, give thanks, break the bread, and give it to these disciples, too.

Luke continues: "And [Jesus] did the same with the cup after supper, saying, 'This cup that is poured out for you is the new covenant in my blood'" (Luke 22:19–20). Like the old covenant at Sinai that was sealed with blood (see Ex 24:5–8), Jesus's blood seals a new covenant through which human beings are saved.

## THE DISCIPLES ON THE ROAD TO EMMAUS

Christ's real presence in Eucharist continues to be Luke's emphasis as he tells the story of the two disciples on the road to Emmaus (Luke 24:13–35). The setting for the account is what we would call Easter Sunday morning. Luke has already told us that the women have discovered the empty tomb and have been told that Jesus is alive. He has been raised. The two disciples on the road have heard this amazing news, but they do not believe it. They are still discouraged; their hopes have been dashed.

As the two disciples walk along, Jesus joins them, but they fail to recognize him. They continue to fail to recognize Jesus as they explain their disappointment to him, as Jesus opens Scripture for them, and as the day's journey ends. Only when they stop for the evening and break bread together do they realize who has been their companion for the whole journey: "When he was at the table with them, he took bread, blessed and broke it, and gave it to them. Then their eyes were opened and they recognized him; and he vanished from their sight" (Luke 24:30–31).

The allusions to Eucharist are obvious in this passage. As we have already noted, Luke used the same language of taking bread, giving thanks, breaking it, and giving it to the disciples when describing the Last Supper. Although Christ was with the disciples when just the two of them were gathered in his name, was with them in the stranger on the road, and was with them in the living word of Scripture, the disciples did not recognize the risen Christ in any of those places. However, they did finally recognize Christ in the breaking of the bread, in Eucharist.

Luke is affirming Christ's presence in Eucharist, but he is also teaching Jesus's disciples, including us, that the Christ whom we receive in Eucharist is also present in these other ways. We must open our eyes and see.

## EUCHARIST IN JOHN

Like Paul and Luke, John teaches that Christ is truly present in Eucharist. Unlike Paul and Luke, John has no account of Jesus's instituting Eucharist during his last meal with the disciples before his death. As we will see, John uses entirely different literary forms to probe the mystery of Christ's presence in Eucharist. In order to understand what John teaches about Eucharist, it will be helpful to have some background knowledge about John's message and method.

The Gospel According to John was written toward the end of the first century to Christians who expected the second coming long before their time and who were asking, "Where is the Son of Man who was supposed to return in glory on the clouds of heaven?" The Gospel is responding to that question by teaching that the risen Christ is not absent, but present. Jesus told his disciples that he would return soon (John 16:16–20), and he did, in his post-resurrection appearances (John 20:19–23). Jesus has never left. He remains with his people in the Church and in what many Christians have come to call the "sacraments." (Some Christians call baptism and Eucharist *ordinances*.)

Instead of having many miracle stories, as do the other Gospels, John tells us about seven *signs*. Each of these stories about the signs is an allegory, that is, each has more than one level of meaning. At one level, the story is about Jesus and his contemporaries. At a deeper level, the story is about the risen Christ in the lives of John's audience, and in our lives.

In addition to his stories of Jesus's mighty signs, John pictures Jesus delivering a number of theological discourses that start as dialogues and end as monologues. In these speeches, Jesus teaches what the stories of the signs teach at the allegorical level.

Because John uses allegory, he wants his audience to know that they should look beyond the literal meaning of his words. Therefore, he teaches his audience how to think metaphorically. He does this by picturing Jesus in conversation with a person who takes Jesus's words too literally. The person's misunderstanding gives Jesus (and John) the opportunity to explain the metaphorical meaning of his words. For instance, Jesus tells Nicodemus that "no one can see the kingdom of God without being born from above" (John 3:3). Nicodemus takes the word *born* literally and says, "How can anyone be born after having grown old? Can one enter a second time into the mother's womb and be born" (John 3:4)? Nicodemus's misunderstanding gives Jesus an opportunity to explain his intent. Jesus was speaking of being born again of "water and Spirit" (John 3:5), of being born again spiritually, not physically.

Jesus tells the woman at the well that he would give her "living water" (John 4:10). She, too, takes the words literally and says, "Sir, you have no bucket, and the well is deep. Where do you get that living water" (John 4:11)? Her misunderstanding gives Jesus the opportunity to explain his real meaning. Jesus was speaking of "water gushing up to eternal life" (John 4:14), of baptism.

A third example: At one point the disciples urge Jesus to eat something. Jesus says, "I have food to eat that you do not know about" (John 4:32). The disciples take the word *food* literally and say, "'Surely no one has brought him something to eat?' Jesus said to them, 'My food is to do the will of him who sent me and to complete his work'" (John 4:33–34).

However, as we shall soon illustrate, when we come to Jesus's discourse on the bread of life, John breaks this pattern. Jesus's listeners are completely repulsed by the literal meaning of his words. Instead of correcting their misunderstanding, Jesus insists on the truth of his statement, causing many to leave him. Jesus's discourse on the bread of life appears after the story of the feeding of the multitude (John 6:1–15), and it explains in depth the allegorical level of meaning (to be explained soon) of this fourth *sign*.

The story of the feeding of the multitude appears in all the Gospels. John appropriates the story and, through subtle changes, gives us signals that he has turned it into an allegory about the presence of the risen Christ in the Church, the risen Christ who feeds his people. Notice that John refers to the Passover: "Now, the Passover, the festival of the Jews, was near" (John 6:4). Remember that the Passover meal was the setting for the institution of Eucharist in Mark, Matthew, and Luke. Notice that it is Jesus who first brings up the subject of feeding the people, not the disciples who, in the other accounts (Matt 14:13–21; Mark 6:30–44; Luke 9:10–17) bring up the subject in order to turn the people away. Notice that it is Jesus himself who feeds the crowds. In the other accounts, Jesus gives the food to the disciples to distribute. Notice that instead of blessing and breaking the bread, Jesus "gives thanks." The Greek (the original language of the Gospel) word for *thanks* is *eucharisteo*. John is giving us plenty of hints that we should look for a deeper meaning, an allegorical meaning, in the story.

So, if we look for a second level of meaning in John's fourth *sign*, the story of the feeding of the multitude (John 6:14), we see that the historical Jesus stands for the risen Christ, the disciples stand for the Church, the crowd stands for those hungry for spiritual nourishment, and the bread stands for Eucharist. Jesus himself distributes the bread because he is the bread of life. It is Jesus who satisfies our spiritual hunger. Notice that there are twelve baskets of bread left over. Twelve stands for the twelve tribes, the twelve apostles, the whole Church. Through this allegory, John is teaching his end-of-the-century audience that Christ is present to them in the Eucharist just as surely as the historical Jesus was present to his contemporaries. Christ is still able to feed his people.

Jesus's "I am the bread of life" discourse (John 6:26–66) that follows the feeding of the multitude teaches the same truth, but through dialogue rather than through allegory. After a lengthy discussion with the crowd, in which Jesus claims to be the bread from heaven, Jesus says, "I am the living bread that came down from heaven. Whoever eats of this bread will live forever; and the bread that I will give for the life of the world is my flesh" (John 6:51).

Jesus's listeners "disputed among themselves, saying 'How can this man give us his flesh to eat?' So Jesus said to them, 'Very truly, I tell you, unless you eat the flesh of the Son of Man and drink his blood, you have no life in you. Those who eat my flesh and drink my blood have eternal life, and I will raise them up on the last day; for my flesh is true food and my blood is true drink. Those who eat my flesh and drink my blood abide in me, and I in them'" (John 6:52–56).

We see, then, that Jesus breaks the pattern that has been established: *Born* was a metaphor for spiritual birth. *Water* was a metaphor for baptism. *Bread* was a metaphor for being nourished by doing God's will. But Jesus seems to insist that the expression *flesh and blood*, which refers to a living person, is not a metaphor, even though this manner of expression upsets his listeners. "Because of this many of his disciples turned back and no longer went about with him" (John 6:66). What is John teaching by telling the story this way?

In John, the words Jesus is pictured as using are *flesh* and *blood*. In Paul, Mark, Matthew, and Luke the words are *body* and *blood*. In every instance, the intent is not to make a scientific statement but a spiritual one. John is teaching his end-of-the-century audience, who are looking for the risen Christ, that Jesus is alive and present in person, the whole flesh and blood person, in Eucharist. When we receive Eucharist, we are not remembering a dead person; we are becoming one with, and being nourished by, a living person: Jesus Christ.

John does not mention Eucharist when he describes Jesus's last meal with his disciples. This last meal is not the Passover meal. In John, Jesus's last meal is the evening before the Passover meal (John 13:1; 19:31), and Jesus, the "lamb of God who takes away the sins of the world" (John 1:29, 36), is killed at the same time that the Passover lambs are being slaughtered for the feast. But, like Paul, John does teach the significance of Eucharist: Those who are disciples of Christ and who have become one with Christ through the Eucharist have a responsibility for others; Christ's disciples are to act as servants for others. After washing the disciples' feet, Jesus says, "Do you know what I have done to you? You call me Teacher and Lord—and you are right, for that is what I am. So if I, your Lord and Teacher, have washed your feet, you also ought to wash one another's feet" (John 13:12b–14).

Although John does not refer to Eucharist at the "last supper" he does, like Luke, refer to Eucharist both at the beginning and end of his Gospel. When John describes Jesus's first sign (see John 2:1–11), he pictures Jesus attending a wedding where he fills empty ablution jars with water that becomes wine. At the allegorical level, a wedding stands for our covenant relationship with God. Ablution jars stand for the law, the previous way of being in right relationship with God. That the jars are empty symbolizes the ineffectiveness of this means of being in right relationship. Jesus has initiated a new spiritual order. Being born into this new spiritual order involves being born again through baptism (water) and Eucharist (wine). Right after this first sign, Jesus tells Nicodemus that in order for a person to enter the kingdom, that person must be born again of water and the Spirit (John 3:5). The dialogue between Jesus and Nicodemus explains the allegorical level of the meaning of this first *sign*.

A reference to Eucharist appears again as Jesus is taken down from the cross. John tells us that one of the soldiers "pierced [Jesus's] side with a spear, and at once blood and water came out" (John 19:34). That blood and water come from Jesus's side symbolize the fact that from the body of Christ, the Church, the body of Christ, is born. Disciples of Christ become one with that body through baptism (water) and Eucharist (blood).

Is Christ present in Eucharist? Is the risen Christ feeding us and accompanying us on our journey? Paul says yes when he reminds the Corinthians: "The cup of blessing that we bless, is it not a sharing in the blood of Christ" (1 Cor 10:15)? Luke says yes when he pictures Jesus placed in a manger, instituting Eucharist at the Passover meal, and has the disciples recognize Jesus in the breaking of the bread. John says yes when he pictures Jesus claiming to be the bread of life that leads to eternal life. While no biblical author uses a word like *transubstantiation* to probe just how Christ is present in Eucharist, inspired biblical authors agree that Christ is present in Eucharist. The Bible does tell me so.

## NOTES

1. Some of the content of this chapter was previously published in Margaret Nutting Ralph, "Catechesis on the Eucharist: New Testament Models," *Catechetical Leader* 22, no. 1 (June 2011), 10–15.

2. Mark's and Matthew's Gospels also give us an account of Jesus's instituting Eucharist at the Passover meal. As we will see, John's Gospel does not.

*Chapter Nine*

# Christ Established a Hierarchical Church

*Does the Bible Tell Me So?*
*Yes: But This Is a Partial Truth*

I have often heard someone in authority dismiss the significance of polls about peoples' convictions regarding certain moral issues by adamantly declaring: "The Church is not a democracy!" It is a matter of fact that the Catholic and Orthodox Churches are not democracies. For instance, Catholics do not elect the Pope, their diocesan bishop, or their parish pastor. The Catholic Church is a hierarchy in that people are ranked one above another according to their authority: Pope, bishops, priests, deacons, and so on. Very often, when someone reminds us that the Church is not a democracy, that person is not only emphasizing the importance of legitimate authority, but is discounting the equally essential role of all the baptized in the body of Christ, the Church.

The Bible does support the idea of legitimate levels of authority in the Church, as we will soon see. However, this duly delegated authority is supposed to be about serving the community and preserving unity, not about power or prestige. At the same time, it is equally true that the Bible supports the idea that individual people are given charismatic gifts, and these, too, are to be used in service to the community. These gifts are not delegated by those in authority, but are given directly by God to the individual.

So, if we acknowledge the God-given role of those in positions they have received through duly delegated authority, the hierarchy in the Church, but ignore the role of the rest of the community that makes up the Church with their God-given charismatic gifts, we are embracing a partial truth, not the whole truth. When we name a partial truth as a whole truth we end up in error.

An example will make this point clear. If we ask, "Why do human beings suffer?" and conclude that human beings suffer because they sin, we have said something true and something that can be supported by Scripture. Sin inevitably leads to suffering. However, if we take this insight as the whole answer to the question regarding human suffering, rather than one true insight, and claim that all suffering is due to sin, we end up in error. Not all suffering is due to sin. This statement can also be supported by Scripture.

In the same way, if we say that Scripture pictures Christ establishing a church that is hierarchical, we are making a true statement in that we can offer evidence from Scripture to support the statement. However, if we claim the hierarchical nature of the Church as the whole truth, we end up in error. All those in the body of Christ, the Church, are priest, prophet, and king. Their gifts, too, are to be recognized and their voices, too, are to be heard.

In this chapter, we will first offer Scriptural authority for the role that hierarchy plays in the Church. We will then examine Scriptural authority for the role that charismatic gifts play in the Church. We will discover that while Christ established a church that has a hierarchy, he did not establish a church that is a monarchy. The whole Church receives the gifts of the Spirit.

## AUTHORITY IN THE GOSPEL
## ACCORDING TO MATTHEW

To offer evidence from Scripture that Christ established a hierarchical church, we will turn first to Matthew's Gospel. Matthew shows a particular interest in establishing Jesus's authority and making it clear that Jesus delegated that authority to the twelve.

The Gospel According to Matthew was written about 80 AD to settled Jewish Christians. Imagine that you are a faithful Jew in 80 AD. Some of your fellow Jews think becoming a disciple of Jesus Christ is being faithful to the Israelites' two thousand year relationship of covenant love with God, and some do not. After all, Jesus was condemned by Jewish authorities, and now Gentiles are becoming disciples of Jesus Christ, and they are not having to obey the Jewish law. Is becoming a follower of Jesus turning one's back on covenant love, or embracing it?

Matthew is teaching his fellow Jews that becoming a disciple of Jesus Christ is being faithful to covenant love because Jesus is the fulfillment of the law and the prophets. Matthew presents Jesus as the new Moses who has authority from God to promulgate a new law. Jesus delegated that authority to his disciples. So, to become a follower of Christ is not to turn one's back on the two thousand year tradition of covenant love that is all important to the Israelite's self-identity. Exactly the opposite is true. For Jews to become disciples of Jesus Christ is for them to remain faithful to covenant love.

Matthew ties Jesus's story to the story of the Israelites by beginning his Gospel with a genealogy that puts the whole story of Jesus in the context of the covenant God made with Abraham: "An account of the genealogy of Jesus the Messiah, the son of David, the son of Abraham" (Matt 1:1). Then, as he tells the story of Jesus's birth, he immediately relates the story to God's covenant promises to God's people. For instance, when Matthew pictures the angel announcing to Joseph that Mary has conceived her child through the Holy Spirit, Matthew says, "All this took place to fulfill what had been spoken by the Lord through the prophet: 'Look, the virgin shall conceive and bear a son, / and they shall name him Emmanuel,' which means, 'God is with us'" (Matt 1:22–23). That the events of Jesus's life "fulfill what has been spoken by the Lord through the prophets" will become a refrain in Matthew's Gospel (see also Matt 2:15; 4:14; 8:17; 12:17; 21:4).

In Matthew's Gospel, Jesus's first major discourse is called the Sermon on the Mount. Matthew places Jesus on a mountain as he delivers a new law to remind his Jewish readers of Moses, who promulgated the first law from a mountain. Jesus is pictured assuring his listeners that he is not abolishing the law and the prophets, but fulfilling them: "Do not think that I have come to abolish the law or the prophets; I have come not to abolish but to fulfill. For truly I tell you, until heaven and earth pass away, not one letter, not one stroke of a letter, will pass from the law until all is accomplished" (Matt 5:17–18).

Jesus then goes on not only to quote various parts of the law, but also to add to the law, making it even more demanding in regard to love of neighbor. For instance, Jesus says, "You have heard that it was said to those of ancient times, 'You shall not murder'; and 'whoever murders shall be liable to judgment.' But I say to you that if you are angry with a brother or sister, you will be liable to judgment. . . . " "You have heard that it was said, 'You shall not commit adultery.' But I say to you that everyone who looks at a woman with lust has already committed adultery with her in his heart" (Matt 5:21–22a, 27–28).

Jesus's words: "You have heard . . . but I say . . . " will also become a refrain in Matthew's Sermon on the Mount. The words highlight Jesus's authority. Who is Jesus to add to the law? On what authority does he speak? He seems to speak on his own authority when he says: ". . . but I say." Where did Jesus get this authority? Matthew focuses on this very question by commenting, "Now when Jesus had finished saying these things, the crowds were astounded at his teaching, for he taught them as one having authority, and not as their scribes" (Matt 7:28).

Jesus's acts of power in healing the sick demonstrate that his words do have authority. This is explicitly stated when Jesus heals a paralytic (Matt

9:2–8). Before healing the man, Jesus forgives him his sins. The scribes take offense, saying, "This man is blaspheming." In their eyes, Jesus is assuming an authority that only God possesses. In response to them, Jesus asserts his authority: "'But so that you may know that the Son of Man has authority on earth to forgive sins'—he then said to the paralytic—'Stand up, take your bed and go to your home.' And he stood up and went to his home. When the crowds saw it, they were filled with awe, and they glorified God, who had given such authority to human beings" (Matt 9:6–8).

Jesus then explicitly delegates his authority to the twelve disciples: "Then Jesus summoned his twelve disciples and gave them authority over unclean spirits, to cast them out, and to cure every disease and every sickness" (Matt 10:1). The twelve are to preach, just as Jesus preaches: "As you go, proclaim the good news, 'The kingdom of heaven has come near'" (Matt 10:7).

Among the twelve, Peter is delegated special responsibility. After Jesus asks his disciples, "Who do people say that the Son of Man is?" Peter responds: "You are the Messiah, the Son of the living God" (Matt 16:13b, 16). In Matthew's Gospel, and only in Matthew's Gospel, Jesus responds to Peter's declaration of faith by saying: "Blessed are you, Simon son of Jonah! For flesh and blood has not revealed this to you, but my Father in heaven. And I tell you, you are Peter, and on this rock I will build my church, and the gates of Hades will not prevail against it. I will give you the keys of the kingdom of heaven, and whatever you bind on earth will be bound in heaven, and whatever you loose on earth will be loosed in heaven" (Matt 16:17–19). Of all of the New Testament passages, these verses state most clearly that Peter had a unique role in the Church and that his role included the authority to bind and to loose. Scripture scholars debate what the power to *bind* and *loose* entails. Suggestions include the authority to exorcise, to legislate, and to teach.

We must also note, however, that the power to bind and to loose is not given just to Peter. When teaching the disciples about how those in the Church should solve disagreements, Jesus tells them, "Truly I tell you, whatever you bind on earth will be bound in heaven, and whatever you loose on earth will be loosed in heaven. Again truly I tell you, if two of you agree on earth about anything you ask, it will be done for you by my Father in heaven. For where two or three are gathered in my name, I am there among them" (Matt 19:18–20). Whatever the power to bind and to loose is, it is not given just to Peter or just to the twelve. It is given to Jesus's disciples, to those who gather in Christ's name.

Soon after describing Jesus giving Peter the "keys to the kingdom of heaven," Matthew once more affirms Jesus's authority in the context of Jewish salvation history by telling the story of the Transfiguration (Matt 17:1–8). Jesus takes Peter, James, and John and goes, again, to a mountain top. Jesus is "transfigured before them, and his face shone like the sun, and his clothes became dazzling white. Suddenly there appeared to them Moses and Elijah, talking with him" (Matt 17:2–3). Moses, of course, promulgated the first law. Elijah was a great prophet. So, Jesus is talking with representatives of the law and the prophets. Peter, still learning the significance of all that is occurring, suggests that he make three tents, one for Jesus, one for Moses, and one for Elijah. To make a tent is to make a tabernacle: a dwelling place. Peter is suggesting that Jesus, Moses, and Elijah should all three continue to dwell with the people. Suddenly, a voice from heaven says, "This is my Son, the Beloved; with him I am well pleased; listen to him" (Matt 17:5).

When you read this passage, put the emphasis on *this* and *him*. "*This* is my Son, the Beloved . . . listen to *him*." The voice saying these words is the voice of God, the same voice that was present at Jesus's baptism. At his baptism, when Jesus came out of the water, he saw "the Spirit of God descending like a dove and alighting on him. And a voice from heaven said, 'This is my Son, the Beloved, with whom I am well pleased'" (Matt 3:16b–17). Matthew is once more teaching his Jewish audience that Jesus did not reject the law and the prophets, he fulfilled them. It is Jesus, not Moses or Elijah, who is to dwell with them. So, to become a disciple of Jesus Christ is to remain faithful to the Jews' two thousand year tradition of covenant love.

As Matthew ends his Gospel, he once more emphasizes for his Jewish audience that the authority that Jesus had, he delegated to his disciples. Once more, a mountain is the setting (Matt 28:16), reminding us of Moses, the Sermon on the Mount, and the Transfiguration. After his resurrection, when Jesus commissions the eleven (Judas's place had not yet been filled), Matthew, and only Matthew, pictures Jesus saying: "All authority in heaven and on earth has been given to me. Go therefore and make disciples of all nations . . . " (Matt 28:18–19a).

So, if I were a Jew who lived in 80 AD, and I read Matthew's Gospel, I would understand that Matthew is teaching that Jesus had God's authority to promulgate a new law. Covenant love has now been extended to all nations, not just to the Israelites. I could become a disciple of Jesus Christ and remain a faithful Jew. I could even accept Gentiles becoming Christian who did not follow the Jewish law. The authority that Jesus had, he delegated to Peter, to the eleven, and to the whole Church. However, the fact that the whole Church has a role is much more evident in other New Testament writings.

## AUTHORITY IN THE GOSPEL
## ACCORDING TO JOHN

The author of John's Gospel had a very different audience than did the author of Matthew's Gospel. As we stated in Chapter 8, John is writing to end-of-the-century Jewish Christians who expected the Son of Man to have already returned on the clouds of heaven and who are asking, "Where is he?" John is encouraging his readers to realize that the risen Christ is in their midst: in the Church, in baptism, in Eucharist, and in all that exists in him and with him and through him.

John's Gospel, in its present form, emphasizes charismatic gifts over duly delegated authority. In fact, the writings from the Johannine community (John's Gospel, and 1, 2, and 3 John) seem to reflect some distrust of authority. Scripture scholars surmise that this distrust comes from their lived experience. The Johannine community is thought to have first been made up of Jews who lived in Palestine and who believed that Jesus Christ was divine. For fellow Jews who did not believe that Jesus was divine, this position was untenable because it seemed to suggest that Yahweh, the transcendent God, was not the only God. Those Jews who did believe in Jesus's divinity were expelled from the synagogues, thus making them vulnerable to persecution by the Romans. The community is thought to have moved to Ephesus. It is here that much of the Gospel According to John was originally written, around 90 AD.

However, John's Gospel shows evidence of editing. For instance, when Jesus gives his long theological discourse during his last meal with his disciples, the discourse has a clear conclusion at the end of Chapter 14 when Jesus says, "Rise, let us be on our way" (John 14:31b). However, the discourse doesn't end there, but continues in Chapter 15

In addition, the Gospel seems to conclude with Chapter 20 when the narrator says: "Now Jesus did many other signs in the presence of his disciples, which are not written in this book. But these are written so that you may come to believe that Jesus is the Messiah, the Son of God, and that through believing you may have life in his name" (John 20:30–31). However, instead of ending, the Gospel continues with a post-resurrection appearance story. Chapter 21 appears to be a later addition.

Scripture scholars believe that these were insertions and additions to the earlier Gospel and date to about 100 AD after the community had gone through a second extremely painful experience.

Evidently, some in the Johannine community not only emphasized Christ's divinity, but emphasized his divinity to the exclusion of his humanity. The community divided over this disagreement. Evidence for the fact that a schism had occurred is present in 1, 2, and 3 John. The author of the letters refers to the dissidents who have left the community as *antichrists*. Due to this division, the community began to better understand the role of delegated authority, which exists to promote unity in the community. The community began to see some value in delegated authority, as long as those who had this authority acted in love.

One way in which John puts less stress on delegated authority is that he does not distinguish between the twelve, the apostles, and the rest of the disciples. The word *apostle* is not used in John's Gospel. John also introduces a character into his Gospel known as *the beloved disciple*, or *the disciple whom Jesus loved*. This unnamed person is often paired with Peter and always seems to understand what is happening before Peter understands. By examining the interaction between Peter and the beloved disciple, we can see how John emphasizes the greatest of all charismatic gifts, love, over authority.

The beloved disciple, who appears in no other Gospel, is present in John for the first time at Jesus's last meal with his disciples. John tells us that at this last meal, Jesus told his disciples that one of them would betray him. "The disciples looked at one another, uncertain of whom he was speaking. One of his disciples—the one whom Jesus loved—was reclining next to him; Simon Peter therefore motioned to him to ask Jesus of whom he was speaking. So while reclining next to Jesus, he asked him, 'Lord, who is it'" (John 13:22–25)?

Here the beloved disciple and Peter are paired for the first time. The beloved disciple is distinguished not by his authority, but by his close, loving relationship with Jesus. Peter does not ask Jesus directly who is going to betray him, but asks the beloved disciple to find out. The beloved disciple appears to be closer to Jesus than is Peter.

Later that evening, Jesus is arrested. Simon Peter and "another disciple," thought by Scripture scholars to be the beloved disciple, follow Jesus. The "other disciple" enters the gate to the courtyard of the high priest with Jesus while Peter stays outside. "So the other disciple, who was known to the high priest, went out, spoke to the woman who guarded the gate, and brought Peter in" (John 18:16). Once in the gate, Peter denies three times being one of Jesus's disciples.

When Jesus is crucified, Peter is nowhere to be seen. However, the beloved disciple is standing at the foot of the cross with Jesus's mother. Jesus, seeing them there, "said to his mother, 'Woman, here is your son.' Then he said to the disciple, 'Here is your mother.' And from that hour the disciple took her into his own home" (John 19:26b–27).

Notice that, just like the beloved disciple, Jesus's mother is never named in John's Gospel. Jesus's mother appears twice in the Gospel, and both times Jesus addresses her as "woman." The first time Jesus calls his mother "woman" is at the wedding feast at Cana (John 2:4). As we discussed briefly in Chapter 8, the story of the wedding feast at Cana is the first of the seven *signs* that John pictures Jesus performing. The story has an allegorical level of meaning.

In the wedding feast of Cana story, Jesus's mother, *the woman*, stands for the Church. The word *woman* is an allusion to Eve in the book of Genesis, the mother of all the living. The Church is the mother of all the living in the new spiritual order that Christ has established. [1]

The two unnamed people who stand at the foot of the cross in John's Gospel, the *woman* and the *beloved disciple*, also have allegorical meaning. The *woman*, once more, represents the Church, the mother of Christ's disciples. The beloved disciple represents all of Christ's beloved disciples who are distinguished by the fact that they love one another. As Jesus had said only a few hours earlier at his last meal with the disciples, "I give you a new commandment, that you love one another. Just as I have loved you, you also should love one another. By this everyone will know that you are my disciples, if you have love for one another" (John 13:34–35).

In the next appearance of the beloved disciple, he is once again paired with Peter, this time in an empty-tomb story. Mary Magdalene has been to the tomb and has found it empty. "So she ran and went to Simon Peter and the other disciple, the one whom Jesus loved, and said to them, 'They have taken the Lord out of the tomb, and we do not know where they have laid him'" (John 20:2).

Peter and the beloved disciple then run to the tomb. The beloved disciple gets there first. However, the beloved disciple does not enter the tomb. He waits for Peter to catch up with him. When Peter arrives, he enters the tomb first. We are told that Peter saw what was in the tomb—the linen wrappings and Jesus's head wrapping in a separate place—but we are not told what, if any, conclusion Peter drew from what he saw. In contrast, John specifically tells us that "the other disciple, who reached the tomb first, also went in, and he saw and believed" (John 20:8).

The beloved disciple represents love. Peter represents authority. A pattern is building in which the person who represents love is consistently reaching the truth before the person who represents authority. Love waits respectfully for authority to catch up, but love gets to the tomb and to the truth first. Love, in the person of the beloved disciple, is the first person, and the only person, to believe before Christ's post-resurrection appearances.

The next pairing of the beloved disciple and Peter occurs in Chapter 21, the section of our canonical Gospel that Scripture scholars surmise was added to the original text some ten years after most of the Gospel was written, after the schism had caused so much pain in the Johannine community. The disciples are fishing in the Sea of Tiberias, but have caught nothing. Jesus appears on the shore and tells them to cast their nets on the right side of the boat. They do as instructed and catch many fish. Then John tells us that the "disciple whom Jesus loved said to Peter, 'It is the Lord'" (John 21:7a). Once more, the person who represents love recognizes Christ before the person who represents authority. Then, Peter rushes to shore, and when they are all assembled, Jesus feeds them with bread and fish.

After the meal, Jesus asks Peter three times, "Do you love me?" Each time Peter professes his love, "Yes, Lord; you know that I love you" (see John 21:15–17). Jesus is giving Peter the opportunity to profess his love as often as Peter has denied knowing him. After each profession of love, Jesus gives Peter responsibility for Jesus's flock. Jesus tells Peter to "feed" his "lambs," to "tend" his "sheep," and to "feed" his "sheep."

Here John is acknowledging that Jesus delegated to Peter a unique responsibility for the Church, much as Matthew does through picturing Jesus saying to Peter, " . . . upon this rock I will build my church." However, in John's account, Peter, who represents authority, has authority only to the extent that his authority is carried out in the context of love. The real sign of being a disciple of Jesus Christ is to love. Duly delegated authority is important and has its role, but it fulfills that role only when it acts in loving service to Christ's Church. Peter is not to rule over his own flock; he is to tend and feed Christ's flock.

## PAUL AND THE EXERCISE
## OF CHARISMATIC GIFTS

We get the clearest picture of the exercise of charismatic gifts when we read Paul's story in the book of Acts. Paul is, arguably, the most influential member of the first-generation church. Seven of the letters in the New Testament were written by Paul, and much of Acts describes how Paul became the apostle to the Gentile world.

Paul received his vocation, not from Peter or one of the twelve, but from the risen Lord. While Paul was on the road to Damascus for the explicit purpose of persecuting those who had become disciples of Jesus, the risen Christ appeared to him and asked, "'Why do you persecute me?' He asked, 'Who are you, Lord?' The reply came, 'I am Jesus, whom you are persecuting'" (Acts 9:4–5). Jesus had chosen Paul "to bring [Jesus's] name before Gentiles and kings and before the people of Israel" (Acts 9:15). That Paul's vocation came directly from God was very important to Paul. As he begins his letter to the Galatians, Paul says, "Paul an apostle,—sent neither by human commission nor from human authorities, but through Jesus Christ and God the Father . . . " (Gal 1:1).

Even though Paul did not receive his vocation from Peter, he did respect Peter's authority. In his letter to the Galatians, Paul says that, after three years, he went to Jerusalem and visited with Peter (see Gal 1:18). Paul believed that "he who worked through Peter making him an apostle to the circumcised also worked through me in sending me to the Gentiles" (Gal 2:8). After fifteen years, Paul went again to Jerusalem. Paul says that "when James and Cephas and John, who were acknowledged pillars, recognized the grace that had been given to me, they gave to Barnabas and me the right hand of fellowship, agreeing that we should go to the Gentiles and they to the circumcised" (Gal 2:9–10).

Paul not only used his charismatic gifts in service to the Church, he encouraged everyone else to do the same. As Paul tells the Corinthians: "Now there are varieties of gifts, but the same Spirit; and there are varieties of services, but the same Lord; and there are varieties of activities, but it is the same God who activates all of them in everyone. To each is given the manifestation of the Spirit for the common good" (1 Cor 12:4–7). Paul encourages the Corinthians to use whatever gifts they have received to serve the Church. They should especially strive for the greatest gift of all: love (1 Cor 13:13).

So, it is true that Christ is pictured in the Gospels as establishing a hierarchical structure in the Church. It is true that over the first century various roles developed that are the roots of the present day roles of bishop, priest (elder), and deacon (see 1Timothy and Titus). However, it is equally true that all of the baptized are given charismatic gifts that they are called to use in service to the community. Just as Christ is priest, prophet, and king, so are all who become one with Christ through baptism. The author of the first letter of Peter describes this great dignity and responsibility of the whole Church when he says: "But you are a chosen race, a royal priesthood, a holy nation, God's own people, in order that you may proclaim the mighty acts of him who called you out of darkness into his marvelous light" (1 Peter 2:9).

## HIERARCHY, NOT MONARCHY

We see, then, that while Scripture supports the idea that Christ established a church that has a hierarchy, necessary to maintain order and unity in the community, Scripture does not support the idea that Christ established a church that is a monarchy. Christ did not establish a form of governance in the Church in which power rests in one person, be it a pope, a bishop, or a priest. Rather, Christ established a church in which the Holy Spirit inspires the whole community, different gifts are given to different people for the good of the whole community, and no part of the body can say to another part of the body, "I do not need you" (see 1 Cor 12:20–21).

Did Christ establish a hierarchical church? Does the Bible tell me so? Yes, but we must not ignore the rest of the story. It is also true that Christ established a church in which the whole community is gifted, and every person, no matter his or her gift, is to use that gift in service to the Church and to the world.

## NOTE

1. It is because Mary is the new Eve that so many statues of Mary have her standing on a snake. Through Christ and the Church (represented by Mary), the result of Adam and Eve's sin has been reversed. Evil has been conquered.

## Chapter Ten

# Scripture Shows a Growing Interest in Mary

*Does the Bible Tell Me So?*
*Yes*

One of the areas of disagreement among Christians is the way in which Mary should be honored in the Church. At one extreme, some Christians seem to regard Mary as someone to be worshipped, as someone more accessible than Christ, as someone who could persuade her son to be on their side. On the other hand, and perhaps in response to such people, other Christians simply ignore Mary, claiming that there is no biblical foundation for many of the claims made on her behalf, such as the immaculate conception (the claim that Mary was born without original sin), the virginal conception (the claim that Mary conceived Jesus through the Holy Spirit), and the assumption (the claim that Mary, body and soul, was assumed into heaven).

As in Chapter 8, when discussing Christ's presence in Eucharist, in this chapter we will not turn to doctrinal formulations to probe the mystery of Mary's unique role in salvation history. Rather, we will turn to the biblical texts and see exactly what they reveal. As we examine the Gospels in the order in which they were written, we will see that the early Church grew in its interest in, and beliefs about, Mary. It is true that the earliest Gospel shows almost no interest in Mary, and the little interest it does show is not complimentary. However, Matthew defends Mary, Luke presents Mary as a person deserving of great honor, and, as we saw in Chapter 9, John presents Mary as a symbol of the Church, the mother of all of Christ's beloved disciples. While not using doctrinal terminology, Scripture does contain the roots of many of the claims made on Mary's behalf.

# MARY IN THE GOSPEL ACCORDING TO MARK

The Gospel According to Mark hardly ever mentions Mary, and when it does, it is in a negative way. Mark's Gospel begins with John the Baptist's witness and the baptism of the Lord. So anything we know about Mary that has to do with Jesus's conception, his birth, or his early years, we did not learn from Mark.

Mary first appears in Chapter 3. Mark tells us that Jesus's mother, brothers, and sisters come to the place where Jesus is preaching and call to him. Those listening to Jesus tell him that his family is outside, wanting to speak with him. Jesus replies, "'Who are my mother and my brothers?' And looking at those who sat around him, he said, 'Here are my mother and my brothers! Whoever does the will of God is my brother and sister and mother'" (Mark 3:33–35).

Since Mark's Gospel does not include any stories surrounding Jesus's birth, such as the annunciation, which would give this passage a wider context, the reader is left with the impression that Jesus simply chose not to respond to his mother, brothers, and sisters. Those to whom he was preaching were more important to him than his family because they were doing the will of God, while his family, presumably, was not.

That this scene pictures some estrangement between Jesus and his family is reinforced by a passage that precedes it. Although Mary is not mentioned specifically, Mark tells us that while Jesus was preaching in his hometown, a great crowd gathered. "When his family heard it, they went out to restrain him, for people were saying, 'He has gone out of his mind'" (Mark 3:21). Mark gives us the impression that Jesus's family didn't understand him, that Jesus knew it, and that he didn't allow this fact to distract him from carrying out his ministry. This impression is confirmed when Jesus later says, "Prophets are not without honor, except in their hometown, and among their own kin, and in their own house" (Mark 6:4).

One other passage in Mark might give us a hint as to why Mary would be treated so dismissively in Mark's gospel. When Jesus returns to his hometown and begins to preach, the people are astounded at his wisdom and his power. They ask, "'Is not this the carpenter, the son of Mary . . . ?' And they took offense at him." (Mark 6:3).

Scripture scholars point out that no other Gospel editor, not even Matthew or Luke, both of whom used Mark as a source, refers to Jesus as "the carpenter, the son of Mary." A son was always referred to as the son of his father, not his mother. Matthew changes the question to "Is not this the carpenter's son? Is not his mother called Mary" (Matt 13:55)? Luke changes it to "Is not this Joseph's son" (Luke 4:22b)? Mark's "Is not this the carpenter, the son of Mary," may well reflect the fact that Jesus's paternity was in question. After all, as we learn in Matthew and Luke, Mary was with child before she and

Joseph began to live together. It appears that Mark's referring to Jesus as Mary's son is a slam at Mary, a person whose virtue was very much in question by those who lived in her hometown.

## MARY IN THE GOSPEL ACCORDING TO MATTHEW

Mary is mentioned for the first time in Matthew's Gospel in his genealogy. The genealogy begins with Abraham and ends with "Jacob the father of Joseph the husband of Mary, of whom Jesus was born, who is called the Messiah" (Matt 1:16). This wording is in contrast to a refrain that appears over and over in the the genealogy that, for each generation, says: " . . . the father of . . . " For instance, the genealogy begins: Abraham was the father of Isaac, and Isaac the father of Jacob, and Jacob the father of . . . " (Matt 1:2). However, Joseph is not called "the father of" Jesus. Rather he is called "the husband of Mary, of whom Jesus was born." This strange change in wording is explained in the next scene: the annunciation to Joseph.

Before turning to Matthew's story of the annunciation, we should note one more interesting and unique fact about Matthew's genealogy. Genealogies usually do not include women. Genealogies trace the male line. However Matthew's genealogy includes four women, in addition to Mary. These women are Tamar, Rehab, Ruth, and Uriah's wife. To include women in a genealogy is so unusual that one cannot but take note and ask, "Who are these women, and why does Matthew include them?"

The four women included in the genealogy are all mothers of sons who were in the male line from Abraham to King David, to Joseph, and all have something questionable about their backgrounds. Tamar, the mother of Perez, seduced her father-in-law, Judah, an ancestor of King David (see Gen 38). Rehab, the mother of Boaz, was a prostitute who helped the Israelites conquer Canaan (see Jos 2, 6:22–26). Ruth, the mother of Obed, was not even an Israelite. She was a Moabite who remained with the Israelites after her first husband died. She remarried and became King David's great-grandmother (see Ruth 4:13–17). Uriah's wife is Bathsheba, the mother of Solomon, the woman with whom David committed adultery before he had her husband killed (see 2 Sam 12:24).

Why did Matthew break convention and include these women in his genealogy? One interpretation is that Matthew is defending Mary's suitability to have been chosen by God. If people in Matthew's audience were thinking: "Jesus can't be the Messiah because he is Mary's son, and God would never have chosen a person with Mary's reputation to be the mother of the messiah," Matthew is pointing out that God had chosen other women who were not admired by their contemporaries to be part of God's saving plan. In the next scene, the annunciation to Joseph, Matthew will not only defend Mary; he will exonerate her. Despite people's opinions, Mary is a person of great virtue.

We never actually meet Mary in Matthew's Gospel, as we do in Luke's. She does not come on stage and speak for herself. There is no annunciation to Mary. However, Mary and her reputation are defended in Matthew because there is an annunciation to Joseph. Joseph is pictured as doubting Mary's virtue, as Jesus's townspeople do in Mark and as, perhaps, Matthew's audience is doing.

Matthew tells us that Mary and Joseph are engaged, but not yet living together, when she is found to be pregnant. Joseph plans to quietly dismiss Mary until an angel appears and tells him that "the child conceived in her is from the Holy Spirit. She will bear a son, and you are to name him Jesus, for he will save his people from their sins" (Matt 1:20b–21). In obedience to the angel of the Lord, Joseph takes Mary into his home.

The birth narratives (a distinct literary form) that appear in Matthew's and Luke's Gospels developed late in the oral traditions that preceded our present Gospels. As explained in our chapter on Eucharist, birth narratives are not responding to the request: "Tell me exactly what happened." They are responding to the request, "Tell me how great this person became as you know from hindsight." The birth narratives are told from a post-resurrection point of view and teach what was understood in the light of the resurrection. They are high Christology stories; that is, they emphasize Jesus's divinity.

The story of the annunciation to Joseph is a high Christology story teaching post-resurrection understandings. This is abundantly clear because, as we have just noted, the angel tells Joseph that Mary "will bear a son, and you are to name him Jesus, for he will save his people from their sins" (Matt 1:21). Jesus's identity and role in salvation history were not understood until after the resurrection.

If we interpret this story as contextualists, as people who consider literary form in order to determine the intent of the inspired author, we can see that the intent of the author is to teach something about Jesus: Jesus is the son of God, a divine person. The human race has been redeemed through Jesus Christ.

However, in the process of teaching Christology, Matthew also teaches Mariology. Mary is the mother of this Jesus, who, in the light of the resurrection, the Church understood to be a divine person. As the understanding of Jesus's identity and of all that had been accomplished through his passion, death, and resurrection grew, so did an interest in Mary. Mary no longer was seen as a woman who lacked virtue but as a person of heroic virtue. It is this Mary that we finally meet in the Gospel According to Luke.

## MARY IN THE GOSPEL ACCORDING TO LUKE

It is in Luke's Gospel that we find more of the roots for the claims that the Catholic Church makes about Mary. This is the case because Luke has much more to say about Mary than does any other Gospel. In Luke's Gospel, the annunciation is not to Joseph but to Mary herself. We meet Mary, hear what the angel says to her and about her, and we hear Mary's faith-filled response. In addition, we read Luke's account of Mary visiting her relative, Elizabeth. These two stories change the context for all that we read about Mary later in Luke's Gospel.

As Luke begins his story of the annunciation, he emphasizes Mary's virtue and her virginity. The angel Gabriel is sent by God to the home of "a virgin engaged to a man whose name was Joseph, of the house of David. The virgin's name was Mary" (Luke 1:27). Next, the greeting of the angel centers our attention on Mary's goodness. The angel says, "Greetings, favored one! The Lord is with you. . . . You have found favor with God" (Luke 1:28b, 30b). When Mary is perplexed by the angel's announcement that she will bear a son, her only question is, "How can this be, since I am a virgin" (Luke 1:34b)? In case any in Luke's audience had doubts about Mary's virtue and her virginity, Luke disabuses them of those doubts immediately.

As in Matthew's annunciation to Joseph, the angel announces to Mary what the Church came to understand about Jesus's identity after the resurrection. Mary will conceive a child whom she is to name Jesus. "He will be great, and will be called the Son of the Most High, and the Lord God will give to him the throne of his ancestor David. He will reign over the house of Jacob forever, and of his kingdom there will be no end" (Luke 1:332–33). Mary will conceive this child through the Holy Spirit. The child born to her "will be holy; he will be called Son of God" (Luke 1:35).

Mary's words to the angel illustrate her loving response to God's favor and model what all of our responses to God's love should be. Mary says, "Here am I, the servant of the Lord; let it be with me according to your word" (Luke 1:38).

Having been told by the angel that her relative, Elizabeth, has conceived a child in her old age, Mary immediately sets out to the hill country to visit her. When Elizabeth sees Mary, Elizabeth's child leaps in her womb and Elizabeth exclaims: "Blessed are you among women, and blessed is the fruit of your womb. And why has this happened to me, that the mother of my Lord comes to me? . . . blessed is she who believed that there would be a fulfillment of what was spoken to her by the Lord" (Luke 1:42b–43, 45).

Elizabeth confirms what the angel also said, that Mary is greatly blessed among all human beings. Mary is not beginning to be blessed because of the angel and Elizabeth's words of greeting. Rather, Mary has always been blessed. God has always been with her.[1] As Elizabeth says, one characteristic of such a blessed person is that she believes that God's promises to her and to her people will be fulfilled. Mary is filled with faith and hope. She is the perfect model of a disciple.

Mary then sings her song of joy and praise: the Magnificat. Again, we see that Mary understands the spiritual order. It is not that Mary will accomplish great things by saying yes to God. Mary continues to see herself as God's servant, and understands that God has done great things for her. Generations will not call her *great*, but *blessed*:

> My soul magnifies the Lord,
> and my spirit rejoices in God my Savior,
> for he has looked with favor on the lowliness of his servant.
> Surely, from now on all generations will call me blessed;
> for the Mighty One has done great things for me,
> and holy is his name. (Luke 1:46–49)

Mary understands her own experience as part and parcel of the experience of her people. God has always had mercy on God's people, from generation to generation. God has chosen the lowly, has cared for them and fed them, just as God has promised through the ages.

> [God] has helped his servant Israel,
> in remembrance of his mercy,
> according to the promise he made to our ancestors,
> to Abraham and to his descendants forever. (Luke 1:54–55)

We see, then, that in Luke, Mary is presented as a model disciple, a person who says yes to God, a person who lives in faith and hope. Because we know this about Mary, when we read a later scene in which Jesus's mother and brothers come looking for him, the scene that we discussed earlier in Mark, Jesus's actions no longer seem dismissive at all. They seem to be naming Mary as a model of discipleship.

The stage is set as it was in Mark (see Mark 3:31–34). Jesus's mother and brothers come, but they cannot reach him because of the crowd. Jesus is told, "'Your mother and your brothers are standing outside, wanting to see you.' But he said to them, 'My mother and my brothers are those who hear the word of God and do it'" (Luke 8:20–21). Luke omits Mark's question, "Who are my mother and my brothers?" as well as the description of Jesus "looking at those who sat around him." In Luke, Jesus doesn't seem to be contrasting his mother and brothers to the disciples, but declaring that they are among his disciples. Mary does the will of God and so is certainly a disciple of her son, Jesus. That this is true reveals a closer bond with Jesus than the bond of their physical relationship.

This interpretation is reinforced by the fact that Jesus says much the same thing later in the Gospel. A woman in the crowd calls out to Jesus and says, "'Blessed is the womb that bore you and the breasts that nursed you!' But he said, 'Blessed rather are those who hear the word of God and obey it'" (Luke 11:27b–28)! Were it not for Luke's including his account of the annunciation to Mary in his Gospel, this response to the woman might seem to be an insult to Mary. However, we know from the annunciation that Mary's response to God is, "Be it done unto me according to your word." Jesus is telling the woman in the crowd that Mary is blessed to be Jesus's mother, but she is even more blessed in that she is a person who hears the word of God and obeys it.

## MARY IN THE ACTS OF THE APOSTLES

Luke's story does not end with Jesus's resurrection. In the Acts of the Apostles, often called the Gospel of the Holy Spirit, Luke tells us how the Spirit descended on the early Church, and how the Church grew throughout the then-known world. Luke tells us that after the ascension, the apostles returned to Jerusalem to await the coming of the Spirit. The apostles "were constantly devoting themselves to prayer, together with certain women, including Mary the mother of Jesus, as well as his brothers" (Acts 1:14).

This same group was together when the day of Pentecost came. Luke emphasizes that the Spirit was received by all who were present: "When the day of Pentecost had come, they were all together in one place. And suddenly from heaven there came a sound like the rush of a violent wind, and it filled the entire house where they were sitting. Divided tongues, as of fire, appeared among them, and a tongue rested on each of them. All of them were filled with the Holy Spirit and began to speak in other languages, as the Spirit gave them ability" (Acts 2:1–4). So, Luke pictures Mary as being present and active when the Spirit descended and empowered the early Church to carry out its mission of proclaiming the good news of Jesus Christ to the entire world.

## MARY IN THE GOSPEL ACCORDING TO JOHN

As we have already explained in Chapter 9, Mary is never named in John's Gospel. We are told that Jesus's mother is present at the wedding feast at Cana (see John 2:1–11) and at the foot of the cross (see John 19:25–27). Both times, Jesus addresses his mother as *Woman*. In both instances, Jesus's mother goes unnamed because, in John, she has become a symbol for the Church.

In the story of Cana, the *Woman* acts as mediator between Jesus and the needs of the wedding guests. The Woman tells Jesus, "They have no wine" (John 2:3b). She then tells the servants to do whatever Jesus tells them to do (see John 2:5b), just as the Church tells all of us to do what Jesus tells us to do. Jesus then fills the empty ablution jars with water that becomes wine, symbols for baptism and Eucharist, the initiation rites for those who will be reborn of water and the Spirit in the new spiritual order that has been established by Christ and that is carried out through the Church.

Jesus's mother, the woman, is also present at the foot of the cross, along with the other unnamed character, the beloved disciple. Here Jesus says to his mother, "Woman, here is your son," and to the beloved disciple, "Here is your mother" (John 19:26b–27a). The Church is the mother of all of Jesus's beloved disciples.

## MARY IN THE BOOK OF REVELATION

Many people think that passages in the book of Revelation speak about Mary. Perhaps one reason for this is that when the Catholic Church celebrates the Feast of the Assumption of Mary into heaven, a passage from the Book of Revelation is read. The Lectionary passage includes the following verses:

> A great sign appeared in the sky, a woman clothed with the sun,
> with the moon under her feet,
> and on her head a crown of twelve stars.
> She was with child and wailed aloud in pain
> as she labored to give birth. . . .
> She gave birth to a son, a male child,
> destined to rule all the nations with an iron rod.
> Her child was caught up to God and his throne. . . .
> Then I heard a loud voice in heaven say:
> "Now salvation and power come,
> and the Kingdom of our God
> and the authority of his Anointed One." (Rev 12:1–2, 5a, 10a)

When the Catholic Church uses these passages from the Book of Revelation to celebrate the feast of Mary's Assumption into heaven, the Church is hearing the words as living words that take on additional levels of meaning in new settings.

To hear Scripture as a living word and to apply it to new settings is a longstanding tradition in the Church. For example, within Scripture, we see the Church apply the suffering-servant songs in Isaiah to Christ. For the original author, the suffering servant was the nation Israel. However, in the light of Jesus's passion, death, and resurrection, the Church found new meaning in the suffering-servant songs, and applied them to Christ.

An example will make this point clear. In Isaiah we read:

> He was oppressed, and he was afflicted,
> yet he did not open his mouth;
> like a lamb that is led to the slaughter,
> and like a sheep that before its shearers is silent,

so he did not open his mouth. (Is 53:7–8)

In the Book of Isaiah, the "he" who is oppressed and afflicted is the nation, Israel, personified. The people are in exile in Babylon, and the prophet, known as 2 Isaiah (Is 40–55), is describing their suffering.

However, in Acts we read that Philip encountered a eunuch who was reading this very passage. The eunuch asks Philip, "About whom, may I ask you, does the prophet say this, about himself or about someone else" (Acts 8:34)? Philip's response to that question was to apply the passage to Jesus Christ. Scripture as a living word takes on new meanings in new settings.

In the same way, the passage from Revelation that the Church proclaims on the feast of the Assumption is not specifically speaking of Mary. In the context of the Book of Revelation, the passage is using archetypal imagery to speak about the ultimate victory of good over evil. The symbol for *good* is the woman clothed with the sun and with the moon under her feet. The symbol for *evil* is a dragon with seven heads and ten horns (see Rev 12:3–4). The dragon wants to devour the woman's child. "But her child was snatched away and taken to God and to his throne" (Rev 12:5b).

The book of Revelation is an example of apocalyptic literature. Apocalyptic literature, a distinct literary form, uses code to send a message of hope to persecuted people. The book of Revelation is assuring Christians who are suffering persecution under Domitian that their persecution will soon be over and that the persecutors will not prevail. Good will win over evil because Christ has already conquered evil and already reigns victorious in heaven.

The symbols can have more than one meaning. So, while the woman represents good, she can also represent the nation of Israel, who gave birth to the savior; Mary, who gave birth to the savior; and the Church, which continues to give birth to the body of Christ, who continues Christ's mission on earth.

In any case, the intent of the author is not to teach the Assumption of Mary into heaven. The intent of the author is to assure his audience, persecuted Christians, that their suffering will soon end because Christ has already conquered evil.

Through the centuries, as the Church grew in her understanding of Mary as the preeminent disciple, the Church began to celebrate about Mary what we believe to be true of all of Jesus's disciples, including ourselves. Just as Jesus passed through death to eternal life, so will Jesus's followers. The Church came to the belief that Mary, as the preeminent disciple, most blessed of all human beings, has already received this great gift. In the light of this belief, the words in the passage from Revelation were understood to express what the Church had come to believe about Mary. It is because this passage from Revelation has been applied to Mary that statues of Mary often picture her standing on a globe and wearing a crown of stars.

# HAIL, MARY, FULL OF GRACE

We see, then, that Scripture reflects a growing interest in and admiration for Mary. That interest and admiration has continued to grow since the biblical canon reached its present form (about the end of the fourth century). However, the Church's understanding of Mary has remained biblically based. When we pray to Mary, we do not address her as a divine person, but as a fellow human being. The prayer most often said to Mary, the *Hail Mary*, reflects this.

The prayer begins, "Hail Mary, full of grace, the Lord is with you." These words are based on Gabriel's greeting to Mary in Luke's story of the annunciation (see Luke 1:28). The prayer continues, "Blessed are you among women, and blessed is the fruit of your womb, Jesus." These words are based on Elizabeth's words to Mary in Luke's story of the visitation (see Luke 1:42).

The prayer concludes, "Holy Mary, mother of God, pray for us sinners now and at the hour of our death." The title "Mother of God" is based on Elizabeth's words to Mary, "And why has this happened to me, that the mother of my Lord comes to me" (Luke 2:43). The prayer then asks Mary to "pray for us," just as disciples of Christ would ask any other dear friend to pray for them. While the Church does claim that Mary is the most blessed of human beings, the Church does not claim that Mary is divine. That claim is reserved for her son, Jesus Christ.

Does Scripture show an interest in Mary? Scripture definitely shows a growing interest in Mary. The Bible does tell me so.

## NOTE

1. It is this belief, that Mary has always been uniquely blessed, that is expressed doctrinally in the words, the "immaculate conception." When speaking doctrinally, the Catholic Church uses St. Augustine's category of thought—original sin—to explain that Mary is most blessed of all human beings: she was conceived without original sin.

# Chapter Eleven

# Only Christians Can Be Saved

## Does the Bible Tell Me So?
## No

Christians disagree on the answer to the question: Can only Christians be saved? Some Christians who are fundamentalists (that is, Christians who do not consider context in order to determine the meaning of biblical passages [see Chapter 1]) say, "Yes, only Christians can be saved." On the other hand, Christians who are contextualists, who do consider context in order to determine meaning, say, "No. God, who is love, did not create all people in God's own image and then offer salvation to only some of God's beloved children."

In this chapter, we will look at some of the passages of Scripture that fundamentalists quote to support their belief that only Christians are saved. We will then look at some of the passages that lead contextualists to believe that all those who seek to do what is right, whether Christian or not, are saved. However, before we turn to the biblical passages on each side of the argument, we should first discuss just what is meant by the word *salvation*.

### WHAT IS SALVATION?

To be *saved* is to be rescued or protected from harm. Christians believe that we have been saved through the life, ministry, passion, death, and resurrection of Jesus Christ. What have we been saved from? We have been saved from slavery to sin; from alienation from self, others and God; and from eternal death. What have we been saved for? We have been set free to become loving people, to live in the kingdom of God, and to enter eternal life. As always, these claims need further explanation.

## SAVED FROM SLAVERY TO SIN

In Chapter 2, when discussing the story of Noah, we looked at the four sin stories in the first eleven chapters of the book of Genesis—the stories of the man and woman in the garden, Cain and Able, Noah and the flood, and the tower of Babel—and explained how they set the stage for the call of Abraham, the beginning of salvation history. Through these stories, the inspired authors are teaching that sin had become so pervasive that human beings were unable to save themselves. Only God could save them. The account of God's beginning to do this starts with God calling Abraham (see Gen 12).

In Chapter 3, we took a close look at the story of the man and woman in the garden. We noted that while this story does not claim to teach history or science, it is teaching something true: sin causes suffering. The suffering incurred by sin includes being alienated from self, God, others, and our world. We also explained that *Adam* is a neuter, collective noun: *Adam* stands for all of us and each of us. We all sin, and we all experience the suffering and alienation that is the inevitable result of sin.

Paul draws on the story of Adam and Eve to provide a contrast as he teaches what has been accomplished through Jesus Christ. That is, Paul turns to the story of Adam and Eve to find a way to image the opposite of Jesus Christ. Adam is a perfect illustration of the pervasive hold that sin had on the human race: referring to the story, Paul says, "Therefore, just as sin came into the world through one man, and death came through sin, and so death spread to all because all have sinned . . . " (Rom 5:12). Paul is explaining that it is because the human race had become slaves to sin that it needed to be saved.

Paul then explains that it is through Jesus Christ that this salvation has been accomplished. Still referring to the story of Adam to provide a contrast to Jesus, Paul says: "For if the many died through the one man's trespass, much more surely have the grace of God and the free gift in the grace of the one man, Jesus Christ, abounded for the many . . . the free gift following many trespasses brings justification. . . . Therefore, just as one man's trespass led to condemnation for all, so one man's act of righteousness leads to justification and life for all" (Rom 5:15b, 16b, 18).

When Paul says, "For if many died through one man's trespass," he seems to be assuming that Adam is a historical person, not a symbol for each human being, for all human beings. Whether or not this is accurate (i.e., whether Paul is expressing a presumption of his time), Paul's teaching is not about Adam, but about Jesus Christ. Paul is teaching that through Jesus, all have been "justified."

To say that human beings have been *justified* is to say that, despite their past sins, they once more have the opportunity to be in right relationship with God. The slate has been wiped clean. The verdict is now, "no longer guilty."

Human beings are free to love God and their neighbor. All of this has been accomplished through Jesus Christ.

## THE KINGDOM OF GOD

Christians believe that, in addition to freeing the human race from slavery to sin, Jesus saved the human race from a consequence of sin: eternal death. Instead, Jesus offered eternal life in the kingdom of God. The kingdom of God was the main topic of Jesus's preaching. Mark and Matthew both picture Jesus beginning his public ministry by teaching about the kingdom of God: "The time is fulfilled, and the kingdom of God has come near; repent, and believe in the good news" (Mark 1:15; see also Matt 4:17). Many of Jesus's parables begin: "the Kingdom of God is like . . ." in order to announce that the in-breaking of the Kingdom of God is central to all that Jesus said and did.

Many people think of the kingdom of God as a place one enters at death. One is in the kingdom when one is in heaven. However, the kingdom that Jesus preached could be present in both this life and the life to come. We see this when Jesus teaches his disciples how to pray. Jesus says:

> Our Father in heaven,
> hallowed be your name.
> Your kingdom come.
> Your will be done,
> on earth as it is in heaven. (Matt 6:9–10)

The lines "Your kingdom come" and "Your will be done" are examples of a device used in Hebrew poetry called *parallel structure*. These lines use *synonymous parallelism*, that is, the second line repeats the thought of the first, but in different words. Jesus is teaching that God's kingdom exists wherever God's will is being done, both on earth and in heaven.

This same idea, that the kingdom of God is not only future, but present, appears in Luke's Gospel. In response to Jesus's teachings about the kingdom of God, some Pharisees ask when the kingdom of God is coming. Jesus tells them: "The kingdom of God is not coming with things that can be observed; nor will they say, 'Look, here it is!' or 'There it is!' For, in fact, the kingdom of God is among you" (Luke 17:20b–21). People living on earth can be living in the kingdom of God.

Perhaps one reason why people think that we are in the kingdom of God only when we enter heaven is that Matthew's Gospel replaces Mark's phrase, *kingdom of God*, with the phrase, *kingdom of heaven*. (Remember, Mark's Gospel was a source for Matthew's Gospel.) For instance, when Matthew pictures Jesus beginning his public ministry, Jesus's first words are not, ". . .

the kingdom of God has come near; repent," as we just saw that they are in Mark, but, "Repent, for the kingdom of heaven has come near" (Matt 4:17).

The reason for this difference in wording is not that Matthew wants to change the concept behind the words. Rather, it is because Matthew is writing for a Jewish audience who believe that the word *God* is too holy to say. So, instead of having Jesus say, "the kingdom of God," Matthew has him say, "the kingdom of heaven." Nevertheless, as we saw in Matthew's *Our Father*, it is clear that, in Matthew's Gospel, too, the *kingdom* can be both "on earth as it is in heaven."

## ETERNAL LIFE IN THE KINGDOM OF GOD

Paul, too, understands the kingdom of God to be present both on earth and in the life to come. This is clear because Paul claims that people enter eternal life, not with physical death, but with baptism. At baptism, we die to sin and join ourselves to the risen Christ, no longer slaves to sin or death. Paul says: "Do you not know that all of us who have been baptized into Christ Jesus were baptized into his death? Therefore we have been buried with him by baptism into death, so that, just as Christ was raised from the dead by the glory of the Father, so we too might walk in newness of life. . . . We know that our old self was crucified with him so that the body of sin might be destroyed, and we might no longer be enslaved to sin" (Rom 6:3–4, 6). In Paul's thinking, eternal life can begin long before one physically leaves earth.

## RECEIVING THE GIFT OF SALVATION

What must we do to accept the invitation to live in the kingdom of God and to receive the gift of eternal life? As we discussed in Chapters 2 and 4, a lawyer asks Jesus this very question. The lawyer asks, "What must I do to inherit eternal life" (Luke10:25b)? When prompted by Jesus to answer his own question, the lawyer says, "'You shall love the Lord your God with all your heart, and with all your soul, and with all your strength, and with all your mind; and your neighbor as yourself.' And [Jesus] said to him, 'You have given the right answer; do this and you will live'" (Luke 10:27–28).

So, when we ask whether only Christians can be saved, we are asking whether only those who consciously believe in, and put their faith in Jesus Christ accept a gift that is offered to all. We have already heard Paul tell us that the gift is offered to all when he taught the Romans that Jesus's "act of righteousness leads to justification and life for all" (Rom 5:18). So the question becomes: If a person does not know Christ, can that person be saved by

Christ? Can a person accept the gift of salvation without realizing that it is through Christ that the gift has been offered?

## WE CAN'T AVOID THE INVITATION

The invitation to the kingdom is not reserved for a chosen few. In Luke's Gospel we read that when Jesus is having dinner at the home of a Pharisee, one of the guests remarks, "Blessed is the one who will eat bread in the kingdom of God" (Luke 14:15)! In response to this statement, Jesus tells the parable of the great dinner (see Luke 14:16–24).

A person gave a great dinner and invited many people. However, when it came time for the guests to come, they made all kinds of excuses to explain why they would not accept the invitation. The master wanted his house full, so he sent out his slave to gather more and more people. Still, the house was not full.

By telling this parable to the guest at the Pharisee's home, Jesus is teaching him, and us, that whether a person is living in the kingdom of God is not a matter of whether that person has been invited. Everyone has been invited. It is a matter of whether the person has accepted the invitation.

## IS NOT KNOWING CHRIST
## REFUSING THE INVITATION?

Some people use Scripture to support their belief that only those who consciously profess Jesus Christ as their savior are accepting the universal invitation to salvation. We will now examine several of the passages used to support this claim. While we will not address all the passages used, we will demonstrate how the contextualist approach to Scripture (see Chapter 1) enables us to address the question: What is the inspired author teaching? In every case, we will see that the inspired author is not responding to the question we are asking. Therefore, we cannot use that author's words to answer our question.

## PAUL'S LETTER TO THE ROMANS

In Paul's letter to the Romans we read: " . . . if you confess with your lips that Jesus is Lord and believe in your heart that God raised him from the dead, you will be saved" (Rom 10:9). With these words, is Paul claiming that those who have not heard the good news of Jesus Christ cannot be saved? He is not. Rather, Paul is teaching the Jewish and Gentile Christians in Rome that they do not earn salvation by obedience to the Jewish law. Rather, they receive salvation as a free gift when they place their faith in Jesus Christ.

Paul is addressing fellow Christians whom he hopes to visit in the near future. His audience is clearly stated in the greeting with which Paul begins his letter: "To all God's beloved in Rome, who are called to be saints: Grace to you and peace from God our Father and the Lord Jesus Christ" (Rom 1:7).

Paul then explains to his fellow Christians, both Jews and Gentiles, that their salvation is received through faith in Jesus Christ, not through fidelity to the law. The whole world needed to be redeemed, Jew and Gentile alike, and the whole world has been redeemed through Jesus Christ. Paul says: "For there is no distinction, since all have sinned and fall short of the glory of God; they are now justified by his grace as a gift, through the redemption that is in Christ Jesus, whom God put forward as a sacrifice of atonement by his blood, effective through faith." (Rom 3:22b–25a). Jewish Christians and Gentile Christians have both received forgiveness for their sins and have been offered the gift of salvation through Jesus Christ.

It is notable in the context of our present discussion that as an example of a person who was saved through faith, not through obedience to the law, Paul uses Abraham. After all, Abraham lived eighteen hundred years before Jesus was born so had no opportunity to place his faith in Jesus. Paul says, "For what does the scripture say: 'Abraham believed God, and it was reckoned to him as righteousness'" (Rom 4:3). Abraham lived before the law was promulgated, and was found righteous even before he was circumcised. So, Paul concludes: " . . . the promise that he would inherit the world did not come to Abraham or to his descendants through the law but through the righteousness of faith" (Rom 4:13).

With this broader knowledge about Paul's letter to the Romans in mind, let us return to the quotation from Paul with which we began, Paul's statement that "if you confess with your lips that Jesus is Lord and believe in your heart that God raised him from the dead, you will be saved" (Rom 10:9). At this point in his letter, Paul is discussing the fate of his beloved fellow Jews who have rejected Christ. His prayer for them is that they may be saved (Rom 10:1). He believes that "seeking to establish their own [righteousness] they have not submitted to God's righteousness" (Rom 10:3). Paul concludes, "For there is no distinction between Jew and Greek; the same Lord is Lord of all and is generous to all who call on him. For, 'Everyone who calls on the name of the Lord shall be saved'" (Rom 10:13).

We see then that Paul is not speaking about the fate of people who do not know Jesus but is insisting that salvation is a gift received by placing one's faith in Jesus Christ, not something earned through obedience to the law.

This teaching is a theme in Paul's letters. He teaches the same truth to the Galatians when he says, "Yet we know that a person is justified not by the works of the law but through faith in Jesus Christ. And we have come to believe in Christ Jesus, so that we might be justified by faith in Christ, and not by doing the works of the law, because no one will be justified by the works of the law" (Gal 2:16). The question we are asking, whether a person who does not know Christ can be saved by Christ, is a completely different question from the faith-versus-works controversy that Paul is addressing.

## WHAT IS "FAITH IN JESUS CHRIST"?

As we have just seen, when Paul presents us with an example of a person who has been justified through faith, not works, the example he chose was Abraham, a person who did not follow the law or know Christ because he lived before the law and before Christ. Yet Paul tells his fellow Christians, both Jews and Gentiles who have had an opportunity to know Christ, that they are saved through "faith in Jesus Christ." What does Paul mean by "faith in Jesus Christ"?

Faith is not the same thing as intellectual assent to doctrine. Rather, when you put your faith in someone, you trust that that person is telling you the truth and that the person will be faithful. People who put their faith in Jesus Christ are people who believe that Jesus is one with God, that Jesus is the revelation of the Father.

Based on who Jesus is, they trust that what Jesus taught them about the kingdom of God is true. As people who have put their faith in Jesus, they live as Jesus has taught them to live. Through baptism they are reborn into a community of fellow believers who also strive to know and do God's will. They enter the kingdom because they have faith that Jesus is the way to the Father. As a result, their prayer in the Our Father is fulfilled in their midst: "Thy kingdom come, thy will be done on earth, as it is in heaven."

Faith does not earn salvation, which is a gift. Rather, faith results in salvation because, by having faith in Jesus, one accepts the gift that Jesus has offered by loving as Jesus has taught us to love. No wonder the early Christians were called *people of the way* (see Acts 9:2). The *way* that Jesus revealed is love of God and love of neighbor.

## THE GOSPEL ACCORDING TO MARK

In Mark's Gospel we read that Jesus, after his resurrection, commissioned his apostles, saying, "Go into all the world and proclaim the good news to the whole creation. The one who believes and is baptized will be saved; but the one who does not believe will be condemned" (Mark 16:15–16). Obviously, this passage is not addressing the question of whether a person who does not know Jesus Christ can be saved by Jesus Christ. In the context of Mark's Gospel, "the one who does not believe" and so will be "condemned" is a person who has rejected the good news after having heard it, not a person who has not yet heard it.

## THE GOSPEL ACCORDING TO JOHN

Many of the passages that are used to support the idea that only those who consciously believe in Jesus Christ can be saved are from the Gospel According to John. While we will discuss only two of these passages, the method we employ to determine the inspired author's intent is applicable to all the passages.[1]

In John, Chapter 3, we read: "For God so loved the world that he gave his only Son, so that everyone who believes in him may not perish but may have eternal life. Indeed, God did not send the Son into the world to condemn the world, but in order that the world might be saved through him. Those who believe in him are not condemned; but those who do not believe are condemned already, because they have not believed in the name of the only Son of God" (John 3:16–18).

To understand what the inspired author is teaching by picturing Jesus saying these words, we must understand the words not only in the context of the plot of John's Gospel, but in the context of the life situation of the author and audience. As we explained in Chapters 8 and 9, the Gospel attributed to John is thought to have been written in the early 90s AD. It is one of a number of books that we have received from what Scripture scholars refer to as the *Johannine community*. These books are the Gospel According to John, the letters 1, 2, and 3 John, and the book of Revelation. By reading all of these books, Scripture, scholars have been able to learn a great deal about the history of the Johannine community.

Remember also that the original members of the Johannine community were Jewish Christians who lived in Palestine. However, their belief that Jesus was a divine person was rejected by their fellow synagogue members because this claim appeared to challenge the core Jewish belief that there is only one God. Therefore, these Christian Jews who insisted on Christ's divinity were expelled from the synagogue. Expulsion from the synagogue was life threatening because Jews in good standing were exempt from emperor worship, but others were not. Those who were expelled from the synagogue became vulnerable to persecution if they refused to honor the emperor as a god. For this reason, the community moved, most likely to Ephesus. John's Gospel is believed to have been written after those who had been expelled from the synagogue by their fellow Jews had been forced to move in order to avoid persecution brought on by their belief in Jesus's divinity.

After the Johannine community moved, the members suffered another terrible blow: they experienced a schism. Some of the members emphasized Christ's divinity to the point that they denied Christ's humanity. These members left the community. This schism caused great pain to the author of 1 John. As we explained in Chapter 9, some additions to John's Gospel, and 1, 2, and 3 John are believed to have been written after this painful schism.

In the context of John's Gospel, the passage we are considering (John 3:16–18) is part of an extended conversation between Jesus and Nicodemus. Nicodemus is "a Pharisee . . . a leader of the Jews" (John 3:1). Nicodemus comes to Jesus to learn who Jesus is. He says, "Rabbi, we know that you are a teacher who has come from God; for no one can do these signs that you do apart from the presence of God" (John 3:2). Nicodemus is open to learning more. Still he misunderstands much of what Jesus teaches him about being born again of water and the Spirit. Jesus says, "Are you a teacher of Israel, and yet you do not understand these things" (John 3:10)? (Remember that the Johannine community had experienced "teachers of Israel" who did "not understand these things" and so expelled their fellow Jews from the synagogue.)

The author then has Jesus explain to Nicodemus the very truths that caused the community to be expelled from the synagogue. Jesus is the Son of God, a divine person who is conscious of his own preexistence. (Remember, John's Gospel begins with a hymn in which the preexistent Word, who was with God and who is God, became flesh and dwelt among us [see John 1:1–14].) Jesus tells Nicodemus: "No one has ascended into heaven except the one who descended from heaven, the Son of Man" (John 3:13). Jesus then continues to tell Nicodemus that "God so loved the world that he gave his only Son, so that everyone who believes in him may not perish but may have eternal life" (John 3:16).

So, when Jesus says that "those who do not believe are condemned already," he is not referring to people who have never heard of him but to people who have heard and seen, but have refused to believe. Therefore, we cannot use this passage, or others like it, as an answer to our question about whether people who do not know Jesus can be saved by him. The author is not addressing our question.

Another passage that is used to claim that only Christians can be saved appears later in John. During his last meal with the disciples before his death, Jesus says, "I am the way, and the truth, and the life. No one comes to the Father except through me" (John 14:6). In this passage, too, the author is teaching that Jesus is divine and is one with the Father. Jesus goes on to say, "If you know me, you will know my Father also. From now on you do know him and have seen him. . . . Whoever has seen me has seen the Father. . . . Do you not believe that I am in the Father and the Father is in me (John 14:7,9,10)?

While this passage claims that all who are redeemed are redeemed through Jesus Christ, it does not claim that one must consciously know Jesus in order to be saved. Perhaps an analogy will make this point clear. As the Gospel of John begins, John claims that everything that exists came into being through the Word that became flesh: "In the beginning was the Word, and the Word was with God, and the Word was God. He was in the beginning with God. All things came into being through him, and without him not one thing came into being" (John 1:1–3).

So, if the Word who became flesh created all that exists, that Word created every person, even if that person is an atheist and does not know God. Likewise, if that Word who became flesh, Jesus, redeemed the whole world, and a person seeks the truth and acts lovingly toward others, Jesus is the source of that person's redemption, even though that person does not know Jesus.

The question is not whether all who are redeemed are redeemed through Jesus Christ. Christians definitely claim that Christ is the source of redemption for all who are redeemed. As we hear Peter preach in Acts: "There is salvation in no one else, for there is no other name under heaven given among mortals by which we must be saved" (Acts 4:12). The question is whether people must be aware that it is Jesus who has won redemption for them in order to accept the gift. As we will now see, there are many passages of Scripture that lead people to believe that Christ's redemptive power extends beyond saving only those who have had the opportunity to know Christ.

## THE UNIVERSALITY OF
## JESUS'S REDEMPTIVE ACTS

As we begin to look at biblical passages that lead people to believe that Jesus's salvific acts are effective in the lives of loving people who do not know Christ, we should note that we have already encountered such passages in previous discussions. When responding to the question, "What is salvation?" we noted that in contrasting the effect of Adam's sin to the effect of Jesus's redemptive acts, Paul says, "Therefore, just as one man's trespass led to condemnation for all, so one man's act of righteousness leads to justification and life for all" (Rom 5:18).

In responding to the question "What must we do to accept the invitation to live in the kingdom of God?" (Luke 10:25b), we noted that a lawyer asked Jesus a question very relevant to the question we are asking: "What must I do to inherit eternal life?" When Jesus asks the lawyer what is written in the law, the lawyer responds: "You shall love the Lord your God with all your heart, and with all your soul, and with all your strength, and with all your mind; and your neighbor as yourself." Jesus tells the lawyer that his answer is correct: "Do this and you will live."

Does this mean that a person who seeks to know and do God's will, and who acts lovingly toward others, but does not yet know Christ, will also inherit eternal life? Might Jesus say those same words to a loving person who does not know him today? Many think that the answer to that question is yes.

Another New Testament passage that seems to support this conclusion is a passage from 1 John that we discussed in Chapter 4: "Beloved, let us love one another, because love is from God; everyone who loves is born of God and knows God. Whoever does not love does not know God, for God is love" (1 John 4:7–8). Admittedly, the author of 1 John is teaching this insight in the context of the revelation received through Jesus Christ, for he then says, "God's love was revealed among us in this way: God sent his only Son into the world so that we might live through him. In this is life, not that we loved God, but that he loved us and sent his Son to be the atoning sacrifice for our sins" (1 John 4:9–10). The author concludes, "No one has ever seen God; if we love one another, God lives in us, and his love is perfected in us" (1 John 4:12).

However, if "love is from God," does this mean that a person who lives in love is, by that very fact, living in union with God, even though that person does not know Christ? We must acknowledge that the author of 1 John is not addressing this question. He is speaking in the context of the Johannine community's schism after some have failed to love by leaving the community. Nevertheless, according to the prologue of John's Gospel, such a love-filled person exists in and through Christ. Has that person also been redeemed by Christ, even though that person does not know Christ?

While none of these passages directly addresses our question regarding salvation for those who lack knowledge of Jesus, one of Jesus's parables does seem to do so. It is the parable of the judgment of the nations (see Matt 25:31–46). This parable is part of Jesus's long eschatological (about the end times) sermon that he is pictured as delivering to his disciples in Matthew's Gospel. In the parable, the nations come before the king to be judged. The king says to those on his right,

> "Come, you that are blessed by my Father, inherit the kingdom prepared for you from the foundation of the world; for I was hungry and you gave me food, I was thirsty and you gave me something to drink, I was a stranger and you welcomed me, I was sick and you took care of me, I was in prison and you visited me." Then the righteous will answer him, "Lord, when was it that we saw you hungry and gave you food or thirsty and gave you something to drink? And when was it that we saw you a stranger and welcomed you, or naked and gave you clothing? And when was it that we saw you sick or in prison and visited you?" And the king will answer them, "Truly I tell you, just as you did it to one of the least of these who are members of my family, you did it to me." (Matt 25:34–40)

In this parable, those who inherit the kingdom are good people who act lovingly toward their neighbor. However, they do not love their neighbor because they recognize Christ in their neighbor. They do not have faith in Jesus and self-consciously follow Jesus's teaching. Faith in Jesus Christ seems to have nothing to do with their actions. They do not understand the relationship between serving their neighbor and serving the king. Nevertheless, the king rewards them. They are called "righteous" by Jesus, who is telling the story, not because of their faith in the king, but because of their loving actions toward others.

Can those who do not know Christ be saved? Scripture leads many thoughtful people to believe that the answer is yes. We know that it is God's will that everyone be saved (see 1 Timothy 2:3). We know that through Christ, the whole world has been reconciled to God, and that all are offered salvation (see Romans 5:18). We know that God is love, and that if we love one another, God lives in us, and God's love is perfected in us (see 1 John 4:12). There are certainly people of other world religions and of no religion who seek the truth and act lovingly toward others. To these beloved children, as well as to Christians, many believe that the king says, "Come, inherit the kingdom prepared for you since the foundation of the world" (Matt 25:34).

Can only Christians be saved? Well, are Christians the only people who live in love? Obviously not. All who live in love can be saved. The Bible tells me so.

## NOTE

1. Among the passages used to proof text that only Christians can be saved are John 3:3–6; 3:16–18; 5:24; 6:28–29; 6:47; 11:25–26; 14:6; 20:31.

*Chapter Twelve*

# The End Is Coming!
# The End Is Coming!

*Does the Bible Tell Me So?*
*Well, It Depends on What You Mean by "The End"*

Throughout history, some people have believed that Scripture prognosticates the end of the world and have tried to read the signs of the times in order to discern when Armageddon, the end time, is upon us. Since we are still here, we know that none of these predictions, including the bubonic plague in the fourteenth century; the plague, great fire of London, and war in the seventeenth century; the fear of the nuclear bomb in the twentieth century; or climate change, blood moons, and volcanoes in the twenty-first century have turned out, in hindsight, to have ushered in the end of the world.

Certainly, some translations of biblical passages use the phrase *the end of the world*. For instance, in the Jerusalem Bible and the King James Bible translations, the disciples ask Jesus, "Tell us, when is this going to happen, and what will be the sign of your coming and of the end of the world?" (Matt 24:3). The New Revised Standard Version translates this same verse: "Tell us, when will this be, and what will be the sign of your coming and of the end of the age?" (Matt 24:3). Other relevant passages (to be discussed) and translations use phrases such as: *the end time, the last days, the last time, the Day of the Lord, the time of the end,* and *the close of the age.*

People who believe that the Bible predicts the end of the world think that biblical passages that warn of coming suffering are prognosticating inevitable events in our present and/or future. They use these passages to instill fear when natural events, such as earthquakes, erupting volcanoes, and eclipses take place. Is what they understand and teach the same as what the inspired biblical authors are teaching us? If not, what misunderstandings lie behind this constantly recurring fear and false prophecy?

As has been true in our discussion of other topics, when we explore this topic, we will see that well-meaning people abuse Scripture and take God's name in vain, thus instilling fear in others, because they fail to read Scripture in context and to ask, "Is the inspired biblical author whom I am quoting addressing the same question I am addressing?"

People who use Scripture to prognosticate the end of the world fail to understand two things: The first is the role of a biblical prophet. The second is apocalyptic thinking and apocalyptic writing. Once more, each of these claims needs further explanation.

## THE ROLE OF A PROPHET

Today's popular understanding of the role of a prophet is not the same as it was in biblical times. The popular understanding is that a prophet has the God-given gift of seeing inevitable future events. Therefore, the prophet can prognosticate (know before) these events and warn us that they are approaching. It is this understanding of prophecy that is held by those who use the Bible to warn others that the end of the world is coming soon. However, the ability to know inevitable future events is not the gift that biblical prophets received from God.

Biblical prophets received the gift of understanding the ramifications of covenant love. That is, they understood that God is love, that God has entered into a mutual relationship of love with God's people, and that this committed relationship carries with it both obligations and ramifications. Therefore, the prophet's message was always one of two things, depending on whether the people were sinning or suffering.

If the people were sinning, the prophet's message was a warning that sin would inevitably result in suffering. However, the warning about suffering was not a prognostication about inevitable future events because, if the people repented, the outcome would be different. We see this pattern in the wonderful, humorous story of Jonah and the Ninevites. The Ninevites were sinning. Jonah warned them that Nineveh would be destroyed. However, once the people repented, the outcome was different, much to Jonah's dismay, since he hadn't wanted to preach to them or to have them be saved in the first place. God was much more loving than Jonah. In the context of covenant love, outcomes change when behavior changes.

However, if the people were not sinning, but suffering, the prophet assured them that all was not lost because God can't stop loving, and God will save them. The day of the Lord will come, the day when God acts powerfully in human history, the day when their present suffering will end. Therefore, the people should remain faithful and live in hope.

As we will see, many of the biblical passages about the end of the world, the end time, the day of the Lord, are messages of hope meant to encourage the people. It is truly an abuse of such passages to use them to frighten people. It is also an abuse of Scripture to claim that these inspired biblical authors were prognosticating the end of the physical world. That is not the subject that they were addressing.

## APOCALYPTIC THINKING

Apocalyptic thinking and apocalyptic literature were prevalent for almost four hundred years, from the time of the persecution of the Jews under Antiochus Epiphanes (who ruled from 175–164 BC) to the time of the second destruction of Jerusalem (135 AD). The movement was born during persecution and rooted in hope. The central idea was that God would intervene in events and overcome evil. The present persecution would end, and God's people would live in a new world order where evil (i.e., the persecutors) no longer reigned.

Jesus lived and taught in the context of this way of thinking. He preached that "the time is fulfilled, and the kingdom of God has come near; repent, and believe in the good news" (Mark 1:15). In other words, a different world order is possible. The kingdom of God, a world in which God's will reigns, is possible. All are invited to repent and live in the kingdom of God.

Jesus is also teaching within the apocalyptic tradition when he says:

> But in those days, after that suffering, the sun will be darkened, and the moon will not give its light, and the stars will be falling from heaven, and the powers in the heavens will be shaken. Then they will see "the Son of Man coming on the clouds" with great power and glory. Then he will send out the angels and gather his elect from the four winds, from the ends of the earth to the ends of heaven. (Mark 13:24–27)

Notice that in this passage, the words "the Son of Man coming on the clouds" is in quotation marks. Jesus is quoting the book of Daniel, one of the two books in the Bible written in the literary form, apocalyptic literature (to be explained; the other book is the book of Revelation).

Jesus is assuring his disciples that even though suffering is in their future and the Temple will once more be destroyed, evil will not prevail. God will send God's messiah, God's anointed one, to save God's people.

## APOCALYPTIC LITERATURE

The book of Daniel, which Jesus is pictured as quoting, is an example of apocalyptic literature. It illustrates the conventions of this kind of writing. One convention is that an author attributes his work to a person who lived generations earlier. The unknown author of the book of Daniel wrote his book during the persecution under Antiochus Epiphanes in the second century BC. However, he attributes his book to Daniel, an Israelite in the Babylonian court. (The Babylonian exile was from 587 BC to 537 BC.)

It is a convention of apocalyptic literature for the author to claim that the person to whom the author has attributed the book (Daniel) has had visions, revelations (the word *apocalypse* means *revelation*, an *unveiling*) in which God revealed the future to him but told him to seal up the content of the visions because the revelation could be revealed only at the end time. That means that the author is describing past events (events from the time of the Babylonian exile until the time of the author) as though they will be future events. The time of the author and audience is the end time when the revelation can be unsealed.

There was nothing misleading to the contemporary audience about using this convention of apocalyptic literature because this way of writing was common to the culture. It was no more misleading than if I were to write a letter to a person whom I do not know and begin, "Dear . . . " The "dear" is not an expression of love, but a convention of the letter form. However, lack of knowledge of this convention of apocalyptic writing has, unfortunately, reinforced some people's misunderstanding that prophets prognosticate inevitable future events.

The point that the author of Daniel is teaching is that God has been in charge of history and remains in charge of history. Evil cannot prevail. The people should live in hope, knowing that their present suffering (the persecution under Antiochus Epiphanes) will end. That is what "the end time" means: the end of the audience's present suffering.

When the author of the book of Daniel describes one of Daniel's visions, in which God intervenes to save God's people, the author says:

I gazed into the visions of the night.
And I saw, coming on the clouds of heaven,
one like a son of man.
He came to the one of great age
and was led into his presence.
On him was conferred sovereignty,
glory and kingship,
and men of all peoples, nations and languages became his servants,
His sovereignty is an eternal sovereignty
which shall never pass away,
nor will his empires ever be destroyed. (Dan 7:13–14; Jerusalem Bible translation)

It is this passage that Jesus quotes when he teaches the disciples about the end times, a passage in which the author of Daniel was teaching that God would intervene in events and send a messiah who would save God's people from their present suffering.

The phrase, "the Son of Man" is the only messianic title that Jesus applies to himself. For instance, Jesus is pictured as referring to himself as *Son of Man* when, after he forgives the sins of a paralytic, he says, "'But so that you may know that the Son of Man has authority on earth to forgive sins,' he said to the paralytic, 'I say to you, stand up, take your mat and go to your home'" (Mark 2:10–12; see also Mark 2:27–28; Luke 19:10; Matt 8:20).

Jesus is also referred to as "Son of Man" when he warns the disciples about his future suffering. In Mark we read, "Then he began to teach them that the Son of Man must undergo great suffering and be rejected by the elders, the chief priests, and the scribes, and be killed and after three days rise again" (Mark 8:31; see also Mark 9:31; 10:33–34; Matt 17:12; 20:18–19; 26:24; Luke 9:22; 18:32–33; 22:22).

In order to understand Jesus's teachings about the kingdom of God and about himself as the Son of Man who will come on the clouds of heaven, we must put them into the context of the time, into the context of apocalyptic thinking. The end time, the day of the Lord, was not some far-off day, two thousand or more years later. The end time was the then-present time, the time when God would intervene in history and save God's people.

## APOCALYPTIC IMAGERY AND NUMEROLOGY

The imagery used in apocalyptic literature is cosmic imagery. When describing the end time, we quoted Jesus as saying, ". . . the sun will be darkened, and the moon will not give its light, and the stars will be falling from heaven, and the powers in the heavens will be shaken" (Mark 13:24–25). Some readers understand this imagery literally and so are frightened by solar eclipses, lunar eclipses, and falling stars. However, these biblical passages are not scientific statements. The imagery is used to teach the profound change in the world order that will occur when the end time comes, when good prevails over evil. To use an English phrase to teach the same thing, I might say that this time of change will be earthshaking. I am not claiming that there will be an earthquake. I am just saying that the world order, as I know it, will change.

Apocalyptic literature also employs numerology. That is, numbers are used in a symbolic way, not in a mathematical or historical way. For instance, in the Book of Revelation, some numbers symbolize incompleteness, and other numbers symbolize completeness. Among the numbers that symbolize incompleteness are any fractions. So, when the author of the book of

Revelation describes the suffering that will occur before the end time as three-and-a-half years (or 42 months, or 1,260 days), he is teaching that the suffering cannot prevail. It will definitely be over soon.

Among the numbers that symbolize completeness are 12 (perhaps because there were 12 tribes and later 12 apostles) and 1,000. One thousand represents magnitude, fullness: 12 times 12 times 1,000 is 144,000. When the author of Revelation pictures 144,000 people sealed as servants of God (see Rev 7:3), the author is not teaching that only 144,000 people are saved, a concrete number. Rather, he is teaching that a multitude is saved, not to mention the additional multitude, too great to count from every nation on earth (see Rev 7:9).

We sometimes use numbers in English phrases to name something other than quantity. For instance, if I said that a man was worried about his yearly evaluation meeting with his boss, but when he came out he was ten feet tall, you would know that I was not describing height, but mood and confidence. Just so, apocalyptic literature uses numbers, not to teach about mathematics or the timing of future events, but to teach beliefs about our covenant relationship with God and God's faithful love.

When we understand the conventions of apocalyptic literature and the ways in which it employs imagery and numerology, we realize that the authors are not threatening terrible future events but are comforting people, are proclaiming good news to people who are already suffering. The good news is that the end time is near. Their suffering will soon be over.

## A PROCESS OF REVELATION

So far, we have considered two of the contexts we need to consider in order to understand what inspired biblical authors are teaching: the context of literary form and the context of the contemporary authors' and audiences' shared beliefs. However, it is just as important to consider the third context: the process of revelation that appears in the overarching narrative of Scripture. In order to do this, we will examine end time passages from various New Testament books in the order in which they were written. We will see that expectations were not always fulfilled by events and that new thinking on issues emerged.

## 1 THESSALONIANS: THE RAPTURE

The earliest writing in the New Testament is Paul's first letter to the Thessalonians, written about 51 AD. In that letter we read this passage:

But we do not want you to be uninformed, brothers and sisters, about those who have died, so that you may not grieve as others do who have no hope. For since we believe that Jesus died and rose again, even so, through Jesus, God will bring with him those who have died. For this we declare to you by the word of the Lord, that we who are alive, who are left until the coming of the Lord, will by no means precede those who have died. For the Lord himself, with a cry of command, with the archangel's call and with the sound of God's trumpet, will descend from heaven, and the dead in Christ will rise first. Then we who are alive, who are left, will be caught up in the clouds together with them to meet the Lord in the air; and so will be with the Lord forever. (1 Thes 4:13–17)

In this letter, Paul, who knew the Thessalonians (see Acts 17:1–9), was responding to a question they had asked: If a person who had become a disciple of Jesus Christ died before Jesus returned on the clouds of heaven, was that person saved, or did that person miss out on joining Christ in heaven?

Paul's answer was good news: that person would still join Christ when Christ returned. In fact, Christ would gather those who had already died before he would gather those who were still on earth. Paul expected to be one of those still on earth. He, along with other disciples of Jesus Christ would be "caught up" ("rapture" [from Latin] is translated as "caught up" in this New Revised Standard Version) and would join the risen Christ in heaven.

In this passage, it is evident that Paul and the Thessalonians expected Christ to come on the clouds of heaven in the near future. Paul expected to still be living on earth when this culminating event occurred. That was Paul's presumption. What Paul is teaching is that even those who die before this culminating event will rise with Christ at the end time.

## JESUS'S ESCHATOLOGICAL DISCOURSE IN MARK

We have already discussed some of Jesus's eschatological (i.e., about the end times) discourse in Mark and how Jesus uses apocalyptic allusions to Daniel and apocalyptic cosmic imagery as he teaches (see Mark 13). We have not yet pointed out that Mark's Gospel, like 1 Thessalonians, teaches the imminence of the expected coming of the Son of Man on the clouds of heaven.

Mark is our earliest Gospel, written about 65 AD, before the destruction of the Jerusalem Temple (70 AD). In this eschatological discourse, Mark pictures Jesus warning the disciples about future suffering before the victory of good over evil. He warns them that the Temple will be destroyed and that they will personally be persecuted. He then says, "So also, when you see these things taking place, you know that he is near, at the very gates. Truly I tell you, this generation will not pass away until all these things have taken place" (Mark 13:29–30).

By 65 AD, the expected time was beginning to pass. Much of Jesus's generation had died. Mark's contemporaries, who were experiencing persecution, were asking just when this hoped-for event was going to occur. In Mark, Jesus adds, "But about that day or hour no one knows, neither the angels in heaven nor the Son, but only the Father" (Mark 13:32). The disciples are warned to stay alert and be always ready since they do not know when this expected event would occur.

## ESCHATOLOGY IN MATTHEW

The Gospel of Matthew dates to about 80 AD, about fifteen years later than that of Mark. Mark is a source for Matthew's Gospel. By comparing the two, we can see how Matthew begins to accommodate to the fact that the end time, the coming of the Son of Man on the clouds of heaven, has not occurred as soon as expected. By now the Temple has been destroyed (70 AD). This event, and Jesus's return on the clouds in glory, while separate events in Mark, seem to be connected. The coming of the Lord will be soon after the destruction of the Temple. Because Jesus has not yet returned in glory, Matthew adds some teachings to Jesus's eschatological discourse that seem to address this unexpected delay.

In one teaching, the theme is to be always ready because no one knows when the Son of Man will come (Matt 24:36–44). Jesus says, "Then two will be in the field; one will be taken and one will be left. Two women will be grinding meal together; one will be taken and one will be left. Keep awake therefore, for you do not know on what day your Lord is coming" (Matt 24:41–42). In this passage, Jesus's coming seems to be more descriptive of individual deaths than of an end of the world.

The importance of constant vigilance is also taught in the parable of the faithful and unfaithful slave (Matt 24:43–51). In this parable, Jesus speaks of a slave who, in his master's absence, does everything that he would do if his master were present. When the master returns, he will realize how trustworthy his slave is and so will put him in charge of all of his possessions. How different this slave is from a slave who, because his master is delayed, abuses those in his charge and acts irresponsibly. When the master does return, that slave will be severely punished.

The theme of always being ready, even when the person to whom one is responsible is delayed in returning, continues in the parable of the ten bridesmaids (Matt 25:1–13) and in the parable of the talents (Matt 25:14–30). In the parable of the wise and unwise bridesmaids, five are wise and bring oil for their lamps, and five are not. When the bridegroom is delayed, they all fall asleep. However, when the bridegroom returns unexpectedly, the wise are able to trim their lamps, welcome him, and accompany him to the wedding banquet. The unwise are not.

The parable of the talents teaches that, while the master is gone, one should not, out of fear, refuse to act. In this parable, a master leaves his slaves in charge of his property. Two slaves please the master by investing his money and returning a profit. One slave is afraid of his master and buries the money. The master praises the two slaves who invested the money, but banishes the one who, out of fear, refused to act.

In addition to adding passages that teach how one should act when the master is delayed, Matthew adds some eschatological signs to his description of Jesus's death and resurrection. Matthew says, "At that moment [i.e., the moment of Jesus's death] . . . the earth shook and the rocks were split. The tombs also were opened, and many bodies of the saints who had fallen asleep were raised. After his resurrection they came out of the tombs and entered the holy city and appeared to many" (Matt 27:51–53). Matthew seems to be suggesting the "already but not yet" aspect of eschatology. Even though the Son of Man has not yet returned in glory on the clouds of heaven, something has radically changed with Jesus's death and resurrection. The "end times," while not complete, have begun.

## ESCHATOLOGY IN LUKE AND ACTS

The Gospel According to Luke and the Acts of the Apostles are part of one work by one author/editor. The author tells us this as he begins Acts by referring to his "first book," the Gospel According to Luke: "In the first book, Theophilus, I wrote about all that Jesus did and taught from the beginning until the day when he was taken up to heaven, after giving instructions through the Holy Spirit to the apostles whom he had chosen . . . " (Acts 1:1–2). Luke's Gospel, too, begins by addressing Theophilus (see Luke 1:3).

Luke, like Matthew, uses Mark as a source. So the author of Luke/Acts, writing in about 85 AD, has the same dilemma that the author of Matthew had: the expectation that Jesus would return on the clouds of heaven during the lifetime of his contemporaries has not been fulfilled as expected. The author of Luke/Acts addresses this dilemma by teaching that Jesus's words were fulfilled through the coming of the Holy Spirit.

Indeed, an emphasis on the Spirit is pervasive in Luke/Acts. For instance, in Mark and Matthew, Jesus begins his public ministry in Galilee by announcing the immanent in-breaking of the kingdom of God (see Mark 1:15; Matt 3:2). In Luke, Jesus's initial preaching in Galilee is about the Spirit of the Lord inspiring him. Jesus quotes from Isaiah, "The Spirit of the Lord is upon me, because he has anointed me to bring good news to the poor . . . " (Luke 4:18a).

Luke's Gospel includes Jesus's eschatological discourse, much as it appears in Mark (see Mark 13; Luke 21), including the understanding that the coming of the Son of Man on the clouds of heaven would take place during the lives of those present (Luke 21:32). But, as Luke continues the story in Acts, Luke pictures Jesus as directing the disciples' attention to the coming of the Spirit. Just before Jesus ascends into heaven, the disciples ask Jesus, "'Lord, is this the time when you will restore the kingdom to Israel?' He replies, 'It is not for you to know the times or periods that the Father has set by his own authority. But you will receive power when the Holy Spirit has come upon you; and you will be my witnesses in Jerusalem, in all Judea and Samaria, and to the ends of the earth'" (Acts 1:7–8).

In the very next chapter, as Luke describes Pentecost, he pictures Peter as explaining that the coming of the Spirit has fulfilled Jesus's eschatological teaching that the end time would be in that generation. In explaining this, Peter quotes the prophet Joel. "In the last days it will be, God declares, that I will pour out my Spirit upon all flesh . . . " (Acts 2:17). This Spirit has been sent by Christ, who now sits at the right hand of the Father in heaven. The Spirit has been poured out on all flesh. Through the Spirit, Jesus is present to his disciples. The expected end time has come.

## ESCHATOLOGY IN JOHN AND
## THE BOOK OF REVELATION

The Gospel of John and the book of Revelation, while not thought to be the work of the same author, are thought to come from the same community, called the Johannine community. These works, in their present form, date to the end of the first century AD.

The Gospel According to John has a different kind of writing from the Synoptic Gospels. John does not repeat the eschatological discourse that Jesus is pictured as giving in Mark, Matthew, and Luke. There are no descriptions of the Son of Man coming on the clouds in glory. For the most part, John's Gospel reflects a realized eschatology rather than a future eschatology. That is, judgment and eternal life are present realities, not future events. For instance, toward the beginning of his public ministry, Jesus is pictured as saying, "Very truly, I tell you, anyone who hears my word and believes him who sent me has eternal life, and does not come under judgment, but has passed from death to life. Very truly, I tell you, the hour is coming, and is now here, when the dead will hear the voice of the Son of God, and those who hear will live" (John 5:24–25).

By the end of the century, many in John's audience were asking, "Where is the risen Christ? He promised to return. Where is he?" John's Gospel is teaching that Jesus did return as promised, his post-resurrection appearances were his return, and Christ has never left. John wants his audience to be able to recognize the presence of the risen Lord in their midst: in all of creation, in the Church, and in what we now call the sacraments. The presence of Christ is not a hoped for future event but a realized present event.

One way in which John teaches that Christ has returned is in the way he describes Jesus's last meal with his disciples and Jesus's later post-resurrection appearance to the disciples. At that last meal Jesus says, "Are you discussing among yourselves what I meant when I said, 'A little while, and you will no longer see me, and again a little while and you will see me?' . . . So you have pain now; but I will see you again, and your hearts will rejoice, and no one will take your joy from you" (John 16:19b, 22).

Jesus does then leave the disciples, is crucified, and dies. They do indeed mourn. However, in a short while, on Easter eve, Jesus appears to the disciples. The disciples are in a locked room when "Jesus came and stood among them and said, 'Peace be with you.' After he said this, he showed them his hands and his side. Then the disciples rejoiced when they saw the Lord" (John 20:19b–20). Jesus promised the disciples that he would return soon and that when he did, their hearts would be full of joy. Jesus did return soon, and their hearts were full of joy. John is teaching his audience that the risen Christ has returned and lives in the midst of his people.

The message of hope in the Book of Revelation is also about the then present, not some distant future. As we mentioned earlier, this work of apocalyptic literature was written during a time of persecution (see Rev 1:9). Its main message is that the people should remain faithful and have hope because Jesus Christ has already overcome evil. In the end, good will prevail. The people's sufferings would end soon.

The book of Revelation departs from some of the conventions of apocalyptic writing that we mentioned earlier. In this book, the author does not attribute his writing to a beloved ancestor in the past but identifies himself as a contemporary of the audience (see Rev 1:9). Therefore, the person who receives the visions (John) is not told to seal up the book until the end time. Rather, he is instructed not to seal up the book because the time is now: "Do not seal up the words of the prophecy of this book, for the time is near" (Rev 22:10b).

The book of Revelation, like other apocalyptic writing, is prophecy in that it offers hope to suffering people, based on an understanding of God's covenant love and God's fidelity to God's people. It is not prognosticating events in our future.

## 2 PETER'S ESCHATOLOGY

Since we began this discussion of eschatology in the context of the process of revelation, beginning with the earliest letter, I Thessalonians, it seems only right to end with a discussion of the letter thought to be the latest letter, 2 Peter, written between 100–125 AD. The unknown author of this letter honored his ancestor in the faith, Peter, by attributing his letter to him, a convention of letter writing at the time.

This letter was written to refute some false teachings. Some people were teaching that, since Jesus had not yet returned on the clouds of heaven as expected, people did not have to worry about judgment. They could just return to their former ways, the sinful lives they had lived before converting to Jesus Christ. These false teachers are asking, "Where is the promise of his coming? For ever since our ancestors died, all things continue as they were from the beginning of creation" (2 Peter 3:4).

The author's response to this false teaching is: "But do not ignore this one fact, beloved, that with the Lord one day is like a thousand years, and a thousand years are like one day. The Lord is not slow about his promise, as some think of slowness, but is patient with you, not wanting any to perish, but all to come to repentance. But the day of the Lord will come, like a thief. And then the heavens will pass away with a loud noise, and the elements will be dissolved with fire. And the earth and everything that is done on it will be disclosed" (2 Peter 3:8–10).

The author of 2 Peter does not respond to the fact that the Son of Man has not yet returned on the clouds of heaven the way Luke does by emphasizing the coming of the Spirit, nor the way John does by emphasizing that Jesus's post-resurrection appearance was a second coming and that Jesus has never left. Rather, in the context of covenant love, he draws the conclusion that God is outside of time, and God is loving. Therefore, people will be held accountable for their actions, there will be a judgment, but God, in God's patience, is postponing that judgment until all hear the good news and choose to live in fidelity to God. This, too, is good news.

## "WORLD WITHOUT END"

Does the Bible prognosticate the end of the world? It does not. The Bible is not addressing scientific questions, but spiritual questions. The Bible does teach us that there will be an end time for each of us (we will all leave earth), and that we are, on a daily basis, held accountable for our choices and our actions. Actions do have consequences. However, the Bible teaches us good news in this regard. We can repent. We can be forgiven. We can die and rise with Christ. We can also recognize Christ's presence in our midst.

As he concludes his Gospel, Matthew teaches that Jesus remains in our midst. Jesus's last words in Matthew picture Jesus assuring his disciples, "I am with you always, even unto the end of the world" (Matt 28:20b; King James Version). Here Jesus is using parallel structure, a literary device in which the same thing is said twice but in different words. The words *always* and *unto the end of the world* are saying the same thing: they are saying *forever*. A similar expression in English might be, *always, until hell freezes over*.

We see, then, that the coming of Christ is a past event, a constantly occurring present event, and a future event. Knowing this good news, we need not listen to doomsayers who abuse Scripture to frighten people about the end of the world. Rather, we can believe the good news that the Bible actually does teach and join the Church in confidently praying: Glory be to the Father, and to the Son, and to the Holy Spirit. As it was in the beginning, is now, and ever shall be, *world without end.* Amen.

# Postscript

There is a core truth that is central to the revelation that Scripture contains: Jesus Christ revealed that God is love. If I have faith in Jesus, I will believe what he taught about the kingdom of God: all are invited to the kingdom. The kingdom is present where God's will prevails. It is God's will that we love one another: no exceptions.

So, whenever the Bible is used to give us permission to marginalize others, to act prejudicially toward others, to feel superior to others, or to exclude others, the person using the Bible in this way is taking God's name in vain. Christians are called to be witnesses of God's love to every person with whom we come in contact, no matter that person's race, religion, sexual orientation, political opinions, or economic situation.

Many people think that in today's world, with modern technology and access to information, everyone has an opportunity to know Jesus Christ and his revelation that God is love. However, this truth is learned primarily through experience. To the extent that we who are Christians fail to love, rather than judge or exclude, every other person, we fail to be witnesses of the good news. We have become walls, rather than pathways, to other people coming to know God and God's love.

How do I know this to be true? The Bible tells me so.

# Bibliography

*Analytical Concordance to the NRSV New Testament*. Grand Rapids, MI: Eerdmans and Oxford, 2000.

Bausch, William J. *A New Look at the Sacraments*. Notre Dame, IN: Fides/Claretian, 1977.

Branick, Vincent P. *Understanding the New Testament and Its Message*. New York: Paulist Press, 1998.

Brown, Raymond E. *An Adult Christ at Christmas: Essays on the Three Biblical Christmas Stories*. Collegeville, MN: Liturgical Press, 1985.

———. *The Birth of the Messiah: A Commentary on the Infancy Narratives in Matthew and Luke*. Garden City, NY: Image Books, 1977.

———. *The Churches the Apostles Left Behind*. New York: Paulist Press, 1984.

———. *The Gospel and Epistles of John: A Concise Commentary*. Collegeville, MN: Liturgical Press, 1988.

———. *An Introduction to the New Testament*. New York: Doubleday, 1997.

Catholic Answers. "Tracts: The Galileo Controversy." 2004. http://www.catholic.com/tracts/the-galileo-controversy.

*The Collegeville Bible Commentary*. Collegeville, MN: Liturgical Press, 1989.

Flowers, Christie. "Christianity's Role in the Battle against Women's Suffrage," May 3, 2007. http://voices.yahoo.com/christianitys-role-battle-against-womens-suffrage-323945.html (site discontinued).

Friedman, Richard Elliott. *Who Wrote the Bible?* New York: Harper and Row, 1987.

Hill, Jim, and Rand Cheadle. *The Bible Tells Me So: Uses and Abuses of Holy Scripture*. New York: Anchor Books/Doubleday, 1996.

Hodge, Bodie. "How Old Is the Earth?" *Answers in Genesis*, May 30, 2007. http://www.answersingenesis.org/articles/2007/05/30/how-old-is-earth.

*Holy Bible: The New Revised Standard Version with Apocrypha*. Nashville: Thomas Nelson Publishers, 1989.

*The Jerusalem Bible*. Garden City, NY: Doubleday, 1966.

John Paul II. "Faith Can Never Conflict with Reason." Pontifical Academy of Sciences. October 31, 1992. http://www.unigre.it/cssf/comuni/documenti/chiesa/Galilei.html (site discontinued).

Knoll, Ray R. *Sacraments: A New Understanding for a New Generation*. Mystic, CT: Twenty-Third Publications, 2006.

*Mercer Dictionary of the Bible*. Macon, GA: Mercer University Press, 1991.

Miller, John W. *How the Bible Came to Be: Exploring the Narrative and Message*. New York: Paulist Press, 2004.

Morrison, Larry R. "The Religious Defense of American Slavery before 1830." *Journal of Religious Thought*. Washington, DC: Howard University School of Divinity, 1980.

*The New Jerome Biblical Commentary*. Englewood Cliffs, NJ: Prentice Hall, 1990.

*The New Layman's Parallel Bible: King James Version; New International Version; Living Bible; Revised Standard Version*. Grand Rapids, MI: Zondervan, 1981.

Nye, Bill, and Ken Ham. "Creationist Debate." National Public Radio (US). 2014. https://www.npr.org/sections/thetwo-way/2014/02/04/271648691/watch-the-creationism-vs-evolution-debate-bill-nye-and-ken-ham.

Ralph, Margaret Nutting. *And God Said What? An Introduction to Biblical Literary Forms*. Mahwah, NJ: Paulist Press, 2003.

———. *The Bible and the End of the World: Should We Be Afraid?* Mahwah, NJ: Paulist Press, 1997.

———. "Catechesis on the Eucharist: New Testament Models." *Catechetical Leader* (June 2011): 10–15.

———. *Plain Words about Biblical Images*. Eugene, OR: Wipf and Stock, 2003.

Stop the Religious Right. "The Bible and Gender Equality." http://www.stopthereligiousright.org/suffrage.htm.

Wikipedia. "Jesus Loves Me." 2014. https://en.wikipedia.org/wiki/Jesus_Loves_Me.

# Biblical Index

# About the Author

**Margaret Nutting Ralph**, PhD, is a teacher, having taught grade school, high school, college, graduate school, and adult education groups throughout the United States, in Canada, Nassau, and Rome, Italy. She worked for the Covington and Lexington Dioceses for thirty years, as a teacher, adult ed. consultant, director of RCIA and Evangelization, and finally as secretary of educational ministries for sixteen years. For twenty-nine years, she served as the director of the MPS (Masters in Pastoral Studies) program for Catholics at Lexington Theological Seminary. Dr. Ralph is the author of eighteen books on Scripture, including Paulist Press's bestsellers *And God Said What?* and the series *Breaking Open the Lectionary: Lectionary Readings in their Biblical Context for RCIA, Faith Sharing Groups and Lectors* (for Cycles A, B, and C of the Lectionary). Her work has been translated into Italian, Spanish, Portuguese, Albanian, and Korean.